Obvious Conduct

Can I Really Behave?

By Mike Van Bruggen

Photo Credit – Cover Photo by Fran Van Bruggen

Published by: www.forwardpublishing.ca

Dedication

Following God can be a lonely walk, but it doesn't have to be an 'alone walk'. In my case, it is not. I dedicate this book to my wife Fran who continues to support and participate with me in life and ministry. After 26 years of marriage, I wouldn't change a thing. Our children, whom we love dearly, have willingly accepted our ministry half a world away. We are thankful for them. We are grateful to all those who have offered encouragement for our ministry. One person comes to mind from our church in Johannesburg. She has relentlessly encouraged me to finish the next chapter, and the book, so she can buy the first copy of Obvious Conduct. So we dedicate the first copy to our dear sister and a great encourager in Christ, Ursula. Then ultimately we desire to give God the glory, praise, and thanks for what HE will allow and enable us to do. Our prayer for this book is that whoever will read it will become an example of the believers in all ways.

Table of Contents

Prologue
A Lack of Understanding

I believe that in the events of human relationships the obvious needs to be stated. The reason that I believe we need to state the obvious is because the obvious may not be obvious to everyone. Then, by definition, it is obvious that the obvious is not always obvious.
–Mike Van Bruggen

We were made with a sense of right and wrong. To some degree, we care what people think of us and how they respond to the things we do. We have an understanding that we are responsible for our behavior. There is an old saying that there is honor among thieves but even criminals instinctively try to hide their crimes.

If we are upstanding citizens and not criminals, our instincts still demand that we hide those things that we know are wrong. I'm talking about things like lying to avoid embarrassment or cheating to win a game. We hide those things to protect our public image and to build up the perception of something we call our character. Character can be defined as the mental and moral qualities that describe or explain us as individual people.

We are all described by our character traits from the earliest times of our lives.

> Proverbs 20:11 says, "Even a child is known by his doings, whether his work be pure, and whether it be right."

When we were in Kindergarten, we all knew who the naughty kids were; we knew who the smart kids were, and we knew who we could trust. We can instinctively detect the character of someone before we get to know them. If children can already perceive and be perceived in this way, how much more can this happen as teens and adults?

If you'll allow me to say it this way, when we trust Jesus as our Savior, we enter 'Spiritual Kindergarten'. We seem to know that there is a character change needed in our lives, yet we have a lack of understanding of how that is accomplished. We see young people doubting their salvation because they still sin. They know themselves by their own doings, and their own doings don't measure up. Like in Kindergarten, spiritually we need to start by learning the basics of behavior that build our character, and then continue to grow from there.

Coming into school implies learning. Coming into Spiritual Kindergarten implies spiritual learning. That's pretty obvious. Due to the confusion of this world, it is not obvious what we should learn and what we should follow. This world is full of ideas; ideas of what we should do and expectations of how we should behave. With a world full of ideas, there are plenty of expectations that contradict. There are more choices than we can evaluate. We need to find the best character traits and follow them.

In the end, there is only one perfect standard that will help us build the best character. After we have placed our faith and trust in Jesus for salvation, we need to yield to the Holy Spirit through the Word of God and let Him change our character to be more like His. Once we enter that Spiritual Kindergarten, we have a choice to remain spiritual toddlers and suffer in doubt and hypocrisy, or we can flourish in real growth and authenticity. As the contents of this book point you to God's book the Bible, let HIS Word guide you to godly character. The result will be: <u>Obvious Conduct: You really can behave!</u>

Chapter One
Growing Abilities

Somewhere in a box, in a cupboard, or in a big drawer, there is a Super 8 movie reel with footage of the day I learned to ride a bike. It is not my very first ride, but as best I can remember, it was the first day I learned to ride. After Dad taught me to balance, and when I was just good enough to get started on my own, he got out the movie camera to immortalize the event. It might be a bit dramatic, but it is a treasured memory.

The movie starts abruptly focusing on me and my takeoff. I had a little red Murry bike; it was the kind that you could put the center bar up or down to make it a boy's or girl's bike. I remember that bike had hard plastic tires like a tricycle, but the training wheels were off, and I was free to ride. I began by riding down the very slight incline of the driveway sidewalk then intentionally, but not smoothly, I turned into the front lawn of our house.

Moving slowly in a sort of wig-wag fashion, I progressed away from the camera across the lawn. I managed to turn and come back across the view of the camera, still wig-wagging, when I realized I had a problem. Dad taught me how to start, but the only way I knew how to stop was to fall off. I remember thinking quickly about an upcoming tree. If I could hit the tree, it would make me stop. The plan was as I stopped (abruptly by hitting the tree), I would put down my feet and smile for the camera. It was all about the show!

The reality was almost as good as the plan. The trunk of the tree was kind of small, maybe about double the width of my plastic tire. I had to maneuver (wig-wag) to hit the tree. Before the impact, in the planning stages, I failed to consider the force of the impact and how that might influence my plans. I had just learned to ride and was not going very fast. Obviously when I hit the tree, my body kept its momentum, and I lunged forward on the bike. No! My face did not hit the ugly tree!

Now, be patient, and let me tell the story... So, with the normal 'cat-like' reflexes of a first grader, I pushed up on the handle bars, somehow pulled up my feet, and jumped off the bike. The bike fell in one direction, and I flew to the other. I landed on my feet and presented myself to the viewing audience. Not quite as graceful as an Olympic athlete, but for a little child, I thought it was pretty good.

Dad thought the whole tree thing was pretty funny. Eventually, I learned to stop. My learning didn't stop. I just learned to stop and put my foot down without the use of any trees, telephone poles, or mailboxes. The Super 8 movie ended in less than a minute, but those moments were the beginning of years of two-wheel fun!

I think everybody I grew up with had at least one bike. As I write this, bike story after bike story comes to mind. While most of them have entertainment value, I will try to stick to stories that demonstrate my growing abilities on two wheel vehicles. I quickly found out that skill and discipline with a bike would enhance my lifestyle. Simple things like being able to turn my head and still ride straight meant that I could see if cars were coming. Once I could look and stop, I could ride my bike on the road to my friend's house (next door). Soon all the basic skills of bike riding were mine.

About this same time in America, there was an entertainment phenomenon emerging under the stage name of Evel Knievel. If you don't know of Evel Knievel, you can do a quick internet search and dozens of articles and videos will pop up. To sum his act up, he was a motorcycle daredevil. He would crash through walls of fire and jump his motorcycle over bigger and bigger things. Every time you would see him on TV, the stunt was bigger and better than the last! His stunts had a big effect on me and the other boys in our neighborhood.

To me, a bicycle and a motorcycle look alike. They don't sound alike, but we could take care of that. Whoever was riding by would hear the rest of us making motorcycle noises, the sounds of shifting gears and skids, and if someone crashed, we made those noises too. With the sights and sounds so similar, it was only natural to think that bicycles could jump things just like motorcycles did. By this time, we all had Sting Rays, big handle bars, banana seats, and sissy bars! They were very good for pulling wheelies. When we got good at wheelies, we progressed, and we built a ramp!

I can remember going over that ramp. It must have been crazy, but that's how I learn. Several things happened that I can remember. Early on, I came down on the front tire, yeah – that's not good, crash city! So, I learned to pull up on the handle bar as I launched off the ramp. Once, I yanked the handle bars right off the bike. I think I broke it on the front wheel landing then pulled it apart on a later jump. I was nicely sailing through the air with no steering ability, yeah – that's not good, crash city. So, then I got my sisters bike (She might not even know until she reads this book, shhhh, don't say anything!). Her bike didn't have Sting Ray handle bars like mine did, so my weight distribution was further forward on the bike. Back then, I never thought of stuff like that. I wish I would have because I was about to experience my second front wheel landing, yeah – that's not good, crash city!

After a few scrapes and bruises, the boys and I figured out that we needed a practice facility. You can see how we were very advanced thinkers for our age. We needed to learn how to land. We had this lake just down the street. There were lots of boat docks, and our ramp was portable. You know what we did... we put the ramp at the end of the dock and went at it. We had to tie a rope to the bike so we could pull it back out of the water. That was real fun and we learned because we would actually grade each jump, if the jump was 'Evel', it was very good.

As time went on, this new skill, and the discipline it took to maintain that skill level, allowed us to jump on dry land. As we got older, we could ride faster and jump farther and higher. We didn't have big things to jump over, so we would line up anything we could find. We would jump over our sports equipment or rocks. Sometimes we would put out a tape measure and try to judge our distance. I wish I could remember how far we could jump. At the time, we had the neighborhood world record committed to memory.

Eventually, we got a minibike (small motorcycle) with a three horsepower engine. We could break all the records with that minibike until we broke the minibike and got in trouble. This I can say; over time, we got pretty good at jumping. We were so confident in our abilities that we began to jump over each other's bikes while standing. We were flying about a high as we were tall, and we could do easy tricks like the BMX bikers of today do. Once we measured my friend's parents' Volkswagen Beetle and concluded that we were jumping high enough and far enough to clear the car, but we could never get the VW Bug to our jump site for a try. My friend's mom didn't like the idea (we should have asked his dad)! On our own scale, we could jump just like a motorcycle daredevil.

For me, it all started there in the front yard, knowing how to start but not knowing how to continue. The 'knowing how' part had to develop, I had to learn. I learned through inspiration and example of someone whose riding skills were better than mine, and I learned through successes and failures. Like most of us, I tried to limit the failures because they hurt. Success felt good, and I wanted to maximize my abilities, so I pressed forward.

For the most part, we find that whatever we do, we try to get better at it. It is simply not satisfying to be stagnant. Looking back on my bike riding experiences, by staying at the beginner or baby level, I would have missed out on a lot of great fun and achievement. Being a 'bike riding baby' never progressing to competence just wasn't an option.

There is something I know about you. Whatever it is that you really do, you do it better now than when you started. Furthermore, you progressed because it was not satisfactory according to your own standards to remain at the 'baby' level. There was no satisfaction with staying stagnant and not growing your skills.

As followers of Jesus Christ, we find that some of the same things apply. There is no satisfaction found by becoming a spiritual baby and never progressing just like there is no satisfaction staying as a bike riding baby. I'm sure my dad was pleased to see me practice and increase my abilities to handle all kinds of different biking situations. So it is with our Christianity, our Heavenly Father is pleased when we practice our Christianity and increase in our abilities to handle all kinds of different situations in a Christlike manner.

We can see from God's Word that it is His intention that we should grow spiritually. 1 Peter 2:2 is an easy place to start.

> 1 Peter 2:2 As newborn babes, desire the sincere milk of the word, that ye may grow thereby:

In order to grow when you're at the baby level of Christianity, you have to learn the basics, the milk of the Word, before you can go on to the bigger things of the faith. There are two quick things to see here.

1. First, growth is expected.
2. Secondly, the growth that is expected is nourished by God's Word.

In 1 Corinthians 3, Paul basically says he is feeding the church at Corinth milk (the basics) because they have not grown and cannot digest the meat (the more advanced teaching). That first day that I rode my bike into the tree, no one would have expected me to jump a minibike nor would they ask me to try. The day I got saved and I started on my Christian walk, no one would have expected me to preach a sermon or write a book. I started, but I had to learn how to continue. I had to work up to that. I had to feed on the milk before I could take in the meat, and the meat led me to maturity.

I looked after and developed the gifts and abilities I received in Christ when He saved me. From a thankful heart, I try to please my heavenly Father with the things that I do. That is the blueprint we need to follow. Paul tells the church at Philippi...

> Philippians 2:12b-13 ...work out your own salvation with fear and trembling. For it is God which worketh in you both to will and to do of his good pleasure.

That phrase "work out your own salvation" means to work it out to completion or maturity. Living it out and growing by experience with the Scripture and Scriptural applications to our lives here on earth. This is a way of God's to include us in His redemptive work to those around us. It is God who works in us to do His pleasure.

It is common for us to use the term 'work out' to signify that we are trying to strengthen our physical body and gain stamina. It is the same concept with our spiritual side. We have to exercise and discipline it to make it strong. Since God chooses to use us in His plan, He wants us to exercise and discipline ourselves spiritually. We benefit by being more useful in His Work.

> Ephesians 2:10 For we are his workmanship, created in Christ Jesus unto good works, which God hath before ordained that we should walk in them.

Our salvation is His workmanship, we are saved "unto good works", and we are to do good and godly things. It was meant from the beginning that we should live our lives in a manner proving to be Christians or Little Christs. To be clear, I am talking about a salvation through faith and trust in Jesus because of His death, burial, and resurrection for the forgiveness of sins. Then after salvation (His workmanship in us), we walk after His example from knowing His Word.

If perhaps you are reading this today, and you don't really know about this salvation and trusting Christ to save you from your sins. Please read **Appendix 1, The Prerequisite**.

I have placed that bonus chapter there just for you! If you're reading this, and you know you're saved, but you want to review the basics of salvation, feel free to take in **Appendix 1, The Prerequisite**.

Everyone else, on to Chapter 2!

Chapter Two
Learning from the Best!

I remember one time my dad's brother and sister came over to the house. Grandma was there too. It was warm outside, summertime, so it must have been my sister's birthday. Dad liked to talk and reminisce, especially when family was around, and Dad had a bunch of bicycle and motor scooter stories from his childhood too. All my dad's brothers and sisters are older than he was. I don't know how it came about, but we learned that my aunt wanted a motorcycle ride. I don't know if we were checking off her bucket list or something. We didn't have bucket lists back then, but at that time, we did have a Honda S-90, and I was happy to take her out for a spin.

What was unknown to me was my aunt didn't know how to ride a bike. That means she didn't know how to balance or lean into the turns. I was planning on taking a little scenic ride, no jumps, no skids, no power slides, and I couldn't really do a wheelie on the S-90. As soon as we took off, I knew she couldn't balance and shift with me on the bike. I was balancing for the both of us. The fact that I had a good amount of practice on all sorts of bikes really kept the experience fun. I had learned from capable teachers and worked out my bike riding skills to the point that I could handle the motorcycle with my aunt and keep her safe.

Here are some silly questions that bring up a good point. What if I had learned to ride from my aunt? What if I'd imitated her on two wheels instead of an accomplished motorcycle daredevil? What if I'd shared her passion for riding rather than the passion for riding of my friends? The answer is I wouldn't have ridden much, and I wouldn't have been very good. I couldn't have taken her for a ride because my ability would not have allowed it. I would still have been a 'bike riding baby' unable to take on the assignment. I have a special memory with my aunt that I would not have if I never learned how to ride well.

What my aunt did very well was live a godly life. She was one of those extended family members that were there from my beginning until she passed on to Heaven at a good old age. We kept in touch. When I got married, and my wife and I had children of our own, we would take them and visit my aunt in the nursing home. During one visit nearing the end of her life on earth, she said something like, "I can't do anything on my own anymore except pray. How can I pray for you?" She was an example of the believers who was beneficial to follow. My aunt (my dad's sister) and my Uncle (my dad's brother) were not only brother and sister but very close friends as well. As I write this book, my uncle is still alive and doing very well. He is at a good old age too. When we are in the States, I try to make it a point to see him. You know what he tells me every visit, "I pray for you every day". Wow, what a treasure! What an example!

You know the thing I need to point out here is, it was not only prayer that my aunt and uncle excelled in; they excelled in every area of their spiritual lives. When I grew older, I ended up working at the same factory where my uncle worked. It was a very big place. When the old timers would find out my last name and figure out that we are related, they would say stuff like, 'If you're half the worker your uncle is, you'll do fine in this company'. I have heard from many people he worked with that he never stretched a 15 minute break into 20, and his 30 minute lunch was exactly that, 30 minutes. My uncle's integrity was unimpeachable; everyone trusted him, and he is an example of the believers.

My aunt and my uncle didn't build that kind of character by being spiritual babies. They exercised their faith and strengthened their abilities. We could say they matured because of their disciplines in the faith. They walked closely with God by knowing His Word, and they lived it out being examples of the believers. When the subject is bike riding, it is much better to imitate and strive after the abilities of an accomplished motorcycle daredevil than my aunt. When the subject is living a life that pleases God and being an example of what authentic Christianity looks like, my aunt and uncle lead the pack as examples.

I know somebody out there is thinking, "That's fine for you Mike, but I don't have those kinds of people in my family". Well, don't let that stop you! There are plenty of godly people out there who would love to help someone grow in their walk with the Lord. I have 'adopted' several moms and dads over the years that walk in godliness! They are people who are exemplary in many areas of their Christian lives. I built relationships and started learning!

My wife Fran and I likewise have adopted many more children who we can share our walk of faith with. When I say adopted, I'm not talking about some legal procedure. I'm talking about striking up the kind of personal relationship that will help others grow and mature in godliness. We build relationships and began sharing!

Proverbs 27:17 comes to mind...

> Iron sharpeneth iron; so a man sharpeneth the countenance of his friend.

We are talking about a God based relationship between two people (or more) that brings about a better awareness in and around them of what God expects. It is a relationship that makes us sharper on the subject of God and how we should walk with Him. Then the relationship can focus in on the application to our lives of what we know God expects. We call this discipleship.

Another definition that I like is this, [1]"Discipleship is teaching someone to be what I already am". A motorcycle daredevil can lead someone to become a motorcycle daredevil, and growing Christian can lead someone to become a growing Christian. The only prerequisite is that you follow someone who is growing in their walk with the Lord and can be the example that we can know, trust, and learn from. Then as we gain more experience and grow in our godly walk, we bring someone alongside us to help them follow God as we do, we become a discipler.

The Apostle Paul tells us as he writes to the church in Corinth, a church that he founded...

> 1 Corinthians 11:1 Be ye followers of me, even as I also am of Christ.

We all need to be disciples, followers of God alongside a more experienced disciple, who is also a follower of God. We all need someone to challenge us with the things found in the Word of God. This is much more than helping us read the words on the pages; this relationship is about how to live out or experience those words from the pages to our lives. This is about making an application from the Bible into our lives with the help of someone else who is doing the same.

The Apostle Paul had several younger men and women whose lives were changed because he invested his life and knowledge of the Word of God into their lives. He helped them become mature in their walk with the Lord. One of the younger guys Paul worked with was named Timothy. Let's take a quick trip through some Scriptures to see Paul's impact on Timothy's life.

Paul and Timothy became directly associated near the beginning of Paul's second missionary journey, somewhere around 50-51AD. We can see the accounting in Acts 16.

Acts 16:1-2 Then came he to Derbe and Lystra: and, behold, a certain disciple was there, named Timotheus, the son of a certain woman, which was a Jewess, and believed; but his father was a Greek: Which was well reported of by the brethren that were at Lystra and Iconium. (Underline Mine)

Timothy is already well thought of among the believers in the churches at Lystra and Iconium. Paul got to know Timothy, and we know that Paul took some time to get to know Timothy's family. It only makes common sense to get to know them before he took Timothy on the missionary journey with him. Paul personally knew them as sincerely faithful, and he mentions memories of Timothy's grandmother Lois, and his mother Eunice.

2 Timothy 1:5 When I call to remembrance the unfeigned faith that is in thee, which dwelt first in thy grandmother Lois, and thy mother Eunice; and I am persuaded that in thee also.

Paul also knows enough about them to be able to say mother Eunice is Jewish while his father is a Greek. From his upbringing, Timothy would be comfortable in either the Jewish or Greek culture, a valuable ability to Paul's ministry outside Jerusalem.

It also appears that Lois, Eunice, and Timothy are already followers of Christ at the time of the Acts 16 visit by Paul. Timothy's family lived somewhere in the area of Derbe and Lystra near Iconium. Most likely Lystra was Timothy's home town. In our terms these cities are in the south central region of modern day Turkey. We can also see from Scripture that Paul had been to this region before. This was recorded in Acts 14.

We see an account from that time. This action packed event happened about 2-3 years earlier during Paul's first missionary journey. Paul and his group came to Iconium. As it became their custom, they would go first into the synagogues and preach the Gospel of Jesus. On this occasion there was a great multitude of Jews and Greeks who believed! There were many more who did not believe, and they stirred up trouble against Paul and his team. Over some time the population of the city became more and more divided over the issue of the Gospel until there was a movement against Paul and his co-workers to try to stone them.

> Acts 14:6-8 They (Paul and his group) were aware of it, and fled unto Lystra and Derbe, cities of Lycaonia, and unto the region that lieth round about: And there they preached the gospel. (Parenthesis Mine)

It is very likely that during these incidents recorded in Acts 14 that Timothy and his family heard and responded to the Gospel message. Therefore, it appears that Timothy had been saved and was beginning to serve, being faithful to the local church. The church leaders in the area had both noticed Timothy and recommended him to Paul and...

> Acts 16:1-3a Then came he (Paul) to Derbe and Lystra: and, behold, a certain disciple was there, named Timothy, the son of a certain woman, which

was a Jewess, and believed; but his father was a Greek: Which was well reported of by the brethren that were at Lystra and Iconium. Him would Paul have to go forth with him; *(Parenthesis Mine)*

Timothy was now traveling with Paul, Silas, and the group as they spread the Gospel message. I suppose you could call this an internship, but we will see this is much more than an internship; this is an intentional real life relationship.

[2]We also see this in the ministry of Jesus Christ. Jesus chose twelve disciples from the group that followed Him...

> Mark 3:14 And he ordained twelve, that they should be with him, and that he might send them forth to preach...

Our Lord Jesus poured His life into these twelve men. This does not minimize the ministry He had with the crowds, but it does show how he spent extended time with His dedicated followers.

Jesus built intentional real life relationships with His disciples and so does Paul, Timothy now being one of Paul's disciples. From Acts 16:4 we see the group traveling from church to church encouraging the believers and reporting on the church directives from Jerusalem. They traveled through the region to the west to Troas on the edge of the Aegean Sea where God called them to cross the sea in to Macedonia, modern day Europe around the northern area of Greece. This is not where the travels end. This is actually the beginning of a 15 to 17 year life-on-life discipling relationship.

By Acts 19:22, we see Paul having enough confidence in Timothy to send him out on his behalf. Timothy is learning and gaining the trust of Paul. Scanning through different passages, we see Timothy described by Paul as a fellow worker or servant in Christ, a beloved son in Christ, a brother in Christ, a fellow teacher of Christ, and a trusted partner[3]. Timothy was growing to the point where he eventually served the church at Ephesus in a pastoral role[4].

Just before Paul's death in Rome, he writes his beloved son in the faith Timothy. Paul knows his end is near, and he wants one last word of encouragement before he is executed. This letter from Paul to Timothy is known to us as 2 Timothy. We find a key verse in the text of 2 Timothy that explains Paul's desire for Timothy and for us. When you see this verse, you will recognize what Paul has been doing with his younger protégé.

> 2 Timothy 2:2 And the things that thou hast heard of me among many witnesses, the same commit thou to faithful men, who shall be able to teach others also.

Timothy, these things we've been doing together for about 17 years, do these things with faithful men who will one day do them again with the next generation. Timothy, you've been the disciple, now step up and be the discipler! Help others grow in their faith as I've helped you so that one day they can do the same for someone else.

2Timothy 2:2 carries a couple of obvious implications. There are disciples and there are disciplers. Disciplers are grown from disciples. Just like I could learn and master two wheel cycling skills from a motorcycle daredevil, I can learn godliness from those who have gone before me and through God's Word. If I am ever going to be a discipler like Paul was, I have to first be a disciple, which just makes common sense.

So here is a very practical truth. If I'm going to be a disciple – (or we can call it being an authentic follower of God?) – I have to know what that looks like. We can look into God's Word and discover the very same principles Paul used with Timothy. We can begin an understanding of Scripture and let it grow in our lives by consistently making application of God's Word in our lives. We can renew our view as to how we see God and the world around us.

This can be the beginning of your close walk with God.

[1]Pushing the Limits, Unleashing the Potential of Student Ministry, Mike Calhoun, Mel Walker, Chapter by Ric Garland, Pg139-148, Thomas Nelson Publishers, Nashville TN

[2]Pushing the Limits, Unleashing the Potential of Student Ministry, Mike Calhoun, Mel Walker, Chapter by Calvin Carr, Pg132, Thomas Nelson Publishers, Nashville TN

[3]Various Scriptures; Romans 16:21, 1Corinthians 4:17, 16:10, 2Corinthians 1:19, Philippians 1:1, 2:19, Colossians 1:1, 1Thessalonians 1:1, 3:2, 2Thessalonians 1:1,

[4]See 1Timothy 1:3, 1Timothy is commonly known as one of the Pastoral Epistles along with 2Timothy and Titus. Each book contains instructions and guidelines for the operation of the Local Church.

Chapter Three
Renew Your View

One of the great things about our neighborhood was that there were several of us that were about the same age, and the plot of land we lived in was just big enough to have a little bit of freedom without getting into too much trouble. There was a bunch of us on my end of the street and another bunch on the other end of the street. They were down by the lake where we would jump our bikes into the water. In between our end of the street and their end of the street was a little hill. The slope on my side of the hill was gentle and easy to ride up on a bike. The slope on the lake side was a bit steeper. You could coast from the top of the hill all the way to the lake about a half mile away.

The problem was that we had to ride all the way back up the hill to go home. By the time we were a little bigger, most of us had 10 speed bikes, and we could use low gear to climb the hill. I realize that most of the bikes today are 18 or 21 speeds, but back then, 10 speeds was about as good as we could imagine. Some of the guys still had small bikes, so even though we could go up easier, we still had to go slow or leave our friends behind.

One day we were down the hill at one guy's house playing with his parachute. It was really not a reliable parachute anymore. It had seen better days. That's why we could play with it. We would hold on to the edges and jump off the small barn in the back, counting on the parachute to land us safely in the back yard. That didn't really work very well. We really didn't think before we did things, but after evaluating our scientific experiments, we concluded that there wasn't enough time to get air underneath the chute. We either had to jump off a much higher roof, or somehow, we had to fill the parachute with air before we jumped. Thankfully, we all lived in one story houses. There were no higher roofs!

However, we did conclude that a slight breeze might fill the chute with air, and once the parachute was full of air, we could safely parachute from the roof top. It was a good theory except it didn't really work. As soon as we would jump, the resistance on the chute changed direction, and we would just drop to the ground. It was a little better because instead of landing on top of the parachute, now the parachute was landing on top of us. We thought this was progress which led us to the next obvious step.

If we could only capture strong enough breezes to actually pull us off the roof, then the tension would be consistent on the chute, the air would stay in the chute, and we would float harmlessly to the ground. I think you can see the progression of thought here. We were learning by taking the new evidence and making an application of it to our reasoning.

Now, you have to know all this could not have happened in one day. For one thing, after a few experimental trials, our ankles would hurt. Also, we had to be very careful about making too much noise because roof jumping wasn't exactly an approved activity within the Mom Society of our neighborhood. The Mom Society had spies all over the place in the form of little brothers and sisters, and our moms all knew each other's phone numbers by heart.

These events happened over several weeks and required the cooperation of the weather man. Finally, the day came when there was a stiff wind coming straight out of the south. Our roof jumping barn had just the right angle. It was now or never! We got out the parachute and hung on for dear life. The chute did pull us off the roof, so instead of us dropping straight down to the ground, we would fly out a few yards away from the barn. It was definitely easier to 'tuck and roll' like the real sky divers of the day used to do.

While that was not the experience we were looking for, the episode did lead us to our next big idea. Remember, we were down the hill with our bikes, we had sore ankles and legs from jumping off the barn, and that hill was between us and some snacks. We reasoned with ourselves noticing that the wind was blowing straight up the road and straight up the hill. We had our bikes, a parachute, and a complementary wind that was heading our way. Can you guess what we did?

Yes! We got on our bikes and held on to the chute. It took us awhile to get the wind into the old parachute; we were kind of flinging it up in the air while holding on to the chute and the bike. That didn't work so well, so we tried riding slowly in unison while stretching the chute across the road... and suddenly the wind caught it, and we took off. When an experiment works, it is a cool thing if only for a brief moment. This idea worked very well. We were rapidly picking up speed!

There was one thing none of us thought of. Once the parachute filled with air, it was so big that we couldn't see where we were going. All I can remember seeing was mailbox after mailbox going by on the side. We were yelling back and forth, "Pull it your way", "Lean out, it's pulling us in". If there would have been a car coming, we wouldn't have known. All we could see was the parachute and our lives flashing before our eyes. This whole thing might have taken fifteen or twenty seconds, and we probably went about three hundred feet. We all crashed, but it seemed like a huge accomplishment!

We put the parachute away, and we agreed that we would just tell the Mom Society that we were scraped and bruised from wrecking our bikes which was kind of true. They would have expected a story like that. It would have been normal. We thought we got away with it but apparently some of those spies told on us. I didn't think my mom knew about the parachute, but many years later Mom was reminiscing and saying something like, "Remember that time you dummies hooked a parachute to your bikes?", and then she laughed out loud! Apparently, the Mom Society had such a good laugh about what happened that we didn't get into trouble.

The wrong things we do and say (along with our misdirected thinking) takes us off course from God. We can label those wrong things and attitudes as "iniquities". It is interesting what the Bible says about our iniquities...

> Isaiah 64:6 But we are all as an unclean thing, and all our righteousness's are as filthy rags; and we all do fade as a leaf; and our iniquities, like the wind, have taken us away. (Underline Mine)

Like the wind in a parachute, we are taken off course. Don't be mistaken; while we were hanging onto the parachute and going up the street, we were not going where we wanted to. We had no control; the wind was taking us away. No matter where that wind was taking us on that day as long as we clung to that chute we were just along for the ride.

Like the parachute full of wind blocked our view of the street, our iniquities block our proper view of God. With the parachute, if there would have been a car, BAM! Maybe we were too close to a mailbox, BAM! We wouldn't have known. If we did not let go when we did, it would have been BAM into something! Without a proper view of God, who knows what harmful thing we are about to run into, BAM! It is a guarantee that without God you will crash.

Now, we have to consider, where do our iniquities take us? To be a little more direct about it, iniquities are sins, and they take us away from God and block our view of how to behave. A wrong activity or a wrong relationship can mean your life is about to suffer a wreck.

It is funny to think about those real life accounts from our childhood. Everyone did silly stuff when they were little. My wife and I like to reminisce and tell stories about our children. It is fun because they were children. We knew they were not thinking like adults and that their reasoning was childish. Children tend to think like children rather than thinking from the more developed mind of an adult. Likewise, mankind tends to think from the standpoint of mankind's own wisdom rather than God's. Stick with me and hear me out.

There is an application here that goes to the bigger, more important things of life. We know what we learn, but what we learn has to be right, or what we know will be wrong. Let me repeat that; read it slowly. We know what we learn, but what we learn has to be right, or what we know will be wrong. There is another "wind" verse in the Bible that I want us to see...

> Ephesians 4:14 That we henceforth be no more children, tossed to and fro, <u>and carried about with every wind of doctrine</u>, by the sleight of men, and cunning craftiness, whereby they lie in wait to deceive (Underline Mine)

We know what we learn, but what we learn has to be right, or what we know will be wrong.

Childish or immature thinking about godliness will be like that wind in the parachute. It will toss you to and fro and carry you into all kinds of false doctrines or teachings. These false teachings can be tricky, and they are carried out by the sleight of men with cunning craftiness. Think about magicians you've seen. They can make you think an egg just came out of your ear or that their beautiful assistant was just sawn in two. It is sleight of hand; it is cunning craftiness. It is deception on the part of the magician for the purpose of entertainment. When it comes to the things that make a useful and godly life, we can't think like children anymore; be mature and grow.

Here is the problem. Most of the world has already been deceived and does not think in a godly way anymore. You might think this is a fairly modern problem, but it is actually not. It is a very original problem. God made mankind starting with Adam (then soon Eve) and placed him in the Garden of Eden. Adam had one basic task; his job was to tend to the garden. Along with the job came one restriction. The restriction was for his good and the good of all who would come after him...

> Genesis 2:16-17 And the LORD God commanded the man, saying, Of every tree of the garden thou mayest freely eat: But of the tree of the knowledge of good and evil, thou shalt not eat of it: for in the day that thou eatest thereof thou shalt surely die.

We would think that if we had only one rule we could keep it. Especially if that rule came directly from God. By Chapter three of Genesis, we see the swirling wind of false doctrine taking our original couple wherever it may. First, we see the cunning craftiness of the serpent lying in wait to deceive...

> Genesis 3:1 Now the serpent was more subtle than any beast of the field which the LORD God had made. And he said unto the woman, Yea, hath God said, Ye shall not eat of every tree of the garden?

The word 'subtle' can be equated with 'elusive'. They are synonyms. The serpent asked questions that were almost true, questions that would raise other questions. Eve began to be discipled by the serpent rather than her husband or God when she entered into his elusive conversation, a conversation that would deliver deception.

> Genesis 3:6-7 And when the woman saw that <u>the tree was good</u> for food, and that <u>it was pleasant</u> to the eyes, and <u>a tree to be desired</u> to make one wise, she took of the fruit thereof, and did eat, and gave also unto her husband with her; and he did eat. And the eyes of them both were opened, and they knew that they were naked; and they sewed fig leaves together, and made themselves aprons. (Underline Mine)

Eve thought it would be good, pleasant, and desirable, but it was that 'every wind of doctrine that deceives' which we were talking about earlier. By the way, Adam joined in as well. All of mankind was deceived and we have been ever since. Mankind bought into a harmful deception and followed a false doctrine.

In the book of Romans, the Apostle Paul talks about this in a little different way. I am noting just three steps in the fall of man.

> Romans 1:21 Because that, when they knew God, they glorified him not as God, neither were thankful; but became vain in their imaginations, and their foolish heart was darkened.

The first step, mankind knew God, but did not glorify or reverence Him; neither were they thankful to Him for the opportunity of their lives. Mankind became vain or futile in their thoughts, viewing life from a selfish, self-centered mindset. Remember Eve saw the benefit of the fruit to her. She was no longer thinking about God nor holding HIM or what He said in high esteem. Mankind was putting no value in knowing or glorifying God. They were showing no reverence for HIM.

> Romans 1:22 Professing themselves to be wise, they became fools,

The second step, now operating from a self-centered mindset rather than a Godly one, mankind is trying to justify their fallen existence by practicing the false doctrines they have bought into. Having falsely reasoned that it would be good for them to take of the forbidden fruit, Adam and Eve did follow through and eat. They became fools even though they believed they would become wiser by ignoring God's Word.

> Romans 1:28 And even as they did not like to retain God in their knowledge, God gave them over to a reprobate mind, to do those things which are not convenient;

The third step, mankind does have a new knowledge but it is a carnal knowledge that does not reflect God or His character. Man is now opposite of what he was created to be. To the extent that mankind does not retain God in their knowledge God gives them over, or allows them to develop, a reprobate mind. The term "reprobate mind" is linked with the thought of being degenerate, debased, immoral, or corrupt. It is without godly principles. The absence of 'retaining God in our knowledge' leads any of us to that same reprobate mindset, and we don't reflect HIS moral character.

The worldliness of the reprobate mindset is sometimes referred to in Scripture as 'the flesh'. When we are walking in a worldly way we are walking in the flesh. The godly mindset that mankind was given at creation is sometimes referred to as 'the Spirit'. This is a reference to the Holy Spirit of God that guides. When we are saved and walking with God, we are said to be walking in the Spirit. The flesh and the Spirit are opposing forces, and none of us can walk in both at the same time. At any given moment, we are walking in one or the other.

Galatians 5:17 For the flesh lusteth against the Spirit, and the Spirit against the flesh: and these are contrary the one to the other: so that ye cannot do the things that ye would.

We've got this problem. We go off course because the influence of the flesh in our lives is outweighing the influence of the Spirit. As saved people, we have this conflict on a daily basis. In theory, we want to follow God, but we wander because we've let the winds of false teaching blow us around until we hardly know which way to go. Then because we've wandered, we wonder why God doesn't give us the answers now that we've wandered from HIS Word. Even though His Word is right there on our book shelf or nightstand, we don't search it. Finally then, because we have wandered far and we are wondering where God has gone, we waste the daily opportunities we have to come closer to God while continuing on with the worldly things we do.

1. We Wander - from God because we have no reverence for God.

2. We Wonder - why God doesn't answer us because we hold no value in His Word.

3. We Waste - the opportunity to come closer because we no longer reflect HIS moral character.

Now we've done all that just to come back where we started.

> Ephesians 4:14 That we henceforth be no more children, tossed to and fro, and carried about with every wind of doctrine, by the sleight of men, and cunning craftiness, whereby they lie in wait to deceive

With a renewed view, we can see that mankind has been messed up for a long time!

Don't be spiritual babies any longer! Don't be tossed to and fro and carried about with every wind of doctrine! Don't be fooled by the trickery of men and of this world! Okay, you might be thinking about the parachute, and the wind taking me wherever it wanted to. I had no control. That is true and valid; I had no control over the chute or the wind. Now, take a moment and think about what I did have control over. Yes, you've guessed it! I had control over my response to what the parachute and the wind were doing in my life. I had the option to let it go and cling to something else that would take me in the right direction.

I didn't have to follow the parachute and we don't have to follow the flesh, the world, or the false teacher's doctrines. Between Ephesians 4:14 and verse 15 there is the contrasting conjunction 'BUT'. The flesh, the world system, and the false teacher's doctrines try to dominate us, 'BUT' there is a choice. It is not a matter of luck or family upbringing, 'BUT' it is your choice what you follow. It is simply your choice.

> Ephesians 4:15 But speaking the truth in love, may grow up into Him in all things, which is the head, even Christ:

Don't be children, 'BUT' grow up (and not only grow up...); grow up into Christ or Christlikeness. The surrounding passage actually speaks about being a part of a healthy body in Christ. Grow up spiritually with a body of believers commonly referred to as a church. Looking at that verse we see the growth coming by the vehicle of truth, God's Word, which is good and proper doctrine. God's Word can help us grow in love, in all things, and into the head which is Christ or Christlikeness.

> 2 Timothy 3:16-17 All scripture is given by inspiration of God, and is profitable for doctrine, for reproof, for correction, for instruction in righteousness: That the man of God may be perfect, thoroughly furnished unto all good works. (Underline Mine)

Perfect there means mature, grown up, prepared, and ready to serve. That is opposite of the reprobate mindset. Don't be like the flesh or the world, 'BUT' be like Christ. Back in our Ephesians 4 text, verses 17-19 rehearse the reprobate mindset and concludes in verse 20 by saying that you didn't learn that worldly stuff from Christ. If we didn't learn that reprobate stuff from Christ or His Word, then where did we learn it? Obviously, we learned from the reprobate mindset of the flesh in this world system.

The key to learning how to behave in a Christlike manner, after we've been messed up by the world, is found in a series of passages that talk about renewal. If we really want to live a life that honors God, growing up into Christlikeness and being mature and able, then we have to learn from the source that will lead us the way we want to go. In this case, we do not want to learn from a motorcycle daredevil; we want to learn from God Himself.

Here is what God, through the pen of the Apostle Paul, says to do...

> Ephesians 4:22-24 That ye put off concerning the former conversation the old man, which is corrupt according to the deceitful lusts; And be renewed in the spirit of your mind; And that ye put on the new man, which after God is created in righteousness and true holiness.

The old man or the sinful man who is corrupt and deceitful is to be put off. Most of the time the analogy here is that of a dirty shirt representing the flesh or the reprobate mindset, and we just take it off. Socially speaking, to be put off means to be shunned. That works too. Remember that mankind has been messed up from the time they ate the fruit of the Tree of the Knowledge of Good and Evil. Put some distance between you and the deceitful teachings that have permeated life on earth since that time.

Secondly, be renewed in the spirit of your mind, or renew your view of the world and see it from a godly perspective.

This godly mindset the opposite of the reprobate mindset we spoke of earlier.

Then, finally, with a new Godly perspective in your mind, put on the new man, or the new ways of a new man after a radical operating system change. Take the operating system of the reprobate mindset out of play and upgrade it with the operating system of a godly mindset. That is not as simple as it sounds. Let's look that over and catch some context.

If we are not careful, we might look at that and say we just need to replace our bad habits or sins with good habits or acceptable behavior. The world has deceitfully outlined a scheme that seems to fit the bill. They might call it Cognitive Behavioral Therapy (CBT) or Habit Reversal Training. This all looks good and the world system can claim some effectiveness in changing some behaviors, but it is not the same as God's good idea. God's plan includes the renewing of the mindset.

Let's say the thing I want to change is this. I eat too many of those little apple pies that they sell in the convenience stores and gas stations. They are by the checkout counter, and I cannot resist them, (actually this is true – I love those things) but they are not good for me. Add to that, that I am a bit 'old school', and I have a problem sticking my credit card into a gas pump without knowing where that information is going; therefore, I like to pay inside, so I can see the attendant while they run the transaction.

Now, you can reason that those little apple pies are there and a good share of the time I pick one up and put it onto the charge. To put it in short form, according to CBT or Habit Replacement Therapy, if I pay at the pump and never go inside, I won't buy the little apple pies, and my problem will be solved. To be sure, I would be avoiding the problem, but I wouldn't be fixing it.

What have I done? I have put a safety on my trigger. I never allow the triggering mechanism to be engaged thereby controlling my urge to buy the pie. I have changed what I do, but I have not changed what I would do. Catch that? I have changed what I do, but I have not changed what I would do. The day that the gas station puts a kiosk out by the pump with little apple pies in it I'll be buying them again. You see, I still love those little apple pies. My mindset has not changed from 'Yummy for my Tummy' to 'Bad for your Belly'.

Now that was a little subtle. Let me go through that again. The world's therapy just changes our trigger mechanisms and never really changes our mindset. We can change what we do to help out but that does not change what we would do when we find ourselves facing one of our triggering mechanisms. When we only change what we do, as soon as a trigger reappears what we would do in response to that trigger will reappear as well. Our mind has not changed and has not been renewed.

I am not saying that it is wrong to avoid your triggers to sin. I am saying that is not the whole answer to the problem. I absolutely believe that an alcoholic who drinks only when they are with certain people needs to stay away from those people until they have a godly mindset renewal. If they only drink when alcohol is present then they should stay away from areas where alcohol is present, until they have had a godly mindset change. *It is the godly mindset renewal that changes what someone would do when the trigger appears.*

In our Ephesians passage, it is that renewal in v23 that is ignored by the deception of the world. Paul also talks about this renewal of the mindset in the book of Romans...

> Romans 12:2 And be not conformed to this world: but be ye transformed by the renewing of your mind, that ye may prove what is that good, and acceptable, and perfect, will of God.

This verse doesn't come into English from the original Greek as well as it could. When Paul says 'be not conformed', it is with the connotation that it is already ongoing. We could maybe say something like 'be not conformed anymore to this world', or 'stop being conformed to this world'. The given here is that the world is influencing us. Then the contrasting conjunction 'BUT' occurs to tell us there is a choice; the same choice we had before. Rather than being conformed to the world, be transformed <u>by the renewing of your mind</u> (or mindset).

Here is what pastor/teacher/writer Warren Wiersbe says about this verse... "The world wants to control your mind, but God wants to transform your mind. This word *transform* (in the original Greek) is the same as *transfigure* in Matthew 17:2. It has come into our English language as the word *metamorphosis*. It describes a change from within. The world wants to change your mind, so it exerts pressure from without. But the Holy Spirit changes your mind by releasing power from within. If the world controls your thinking, you are a *conformer*; if God controls your mind, you are a *transformer*.[1]" This transformation comes and shows that good and acceptable will of God in the transformer's life. I know many of you always wanted to be a transformer; here's your chance!

Now, we see that the renewing of the mindset that we want is an inside-out metamorphosis. Like a caterpillar that weaves itself into a cocoon, from inside the cocoon, the caterpillar becomes a butterfly. It goes from a crawling wormy thing to a beautiful butterfly. The renewing of the mind and the new mindset that comes after the reprobate mind and mindset is transformed through metamorphosis.

We have an indication from Romans 12:2 that the product of the renewed mind is godliness. We see there is a change from worldliness to godliness, but what exactly is the agent of change? We can't leave anything this important to chance. If we use the wrong changing agent, we will get the wrong result. We might become a motorcycle daredevil or a paratrooper.

Fortunately, we don't have to guess. Our next passage gives us the answer.

> Colossians 3:9b-10 ...seeing that ye have put off the old man with his deeds; And have put on the new

man, <u>which is renewed in knowledge after the image of Him that created him</u> (Underline Mine)

We see some familiar words and phrases here: *put off, put on, and renewed*. Carrying through from the previous passages, we are putting off the old reprobate man and putting on the new or renewed man. We see the key to the change right here; renewed in the knowledge after the image of Him (God). Coming into a likeness or image of God through knowledge of HIM is the renewal. Recapping from the start, we put off the old reprobate man and mindset. We renew or transform from the old reprobate mindset to the new godly mindset through an internal metamorphosis, a metamorphosis that is guided by the agent of change which is the knowledge of God causing a likeness to God. We could summarize that by saying 'growing up into Christlikeness in all things'.

With the knowledge of God that produces Christlikeness identified as the agent of change that causes the inside-out metamorphosis, we have only one question left to answer in this chapter. Where do we get this knowledge of God?

> Psalm 119:9 Wherewithal shall a young man cleanse his way? by taking heed thereto according to thy word.

It is the Word of God that does this cleansing, this inside-out metamorphosis that brings us to the new godly mindset. We must take heed or pay attention to the Word of God, our reliable Scriptures that we call the Bible. I spend a great deal of time establishing the reliability of the Bible as the holy inspired Word of God in my book, 'Obvious Choices: Can I Really Believe?'. In that book we see, "Since we can obviously conclude the Bible is accurate and that the only explanation of its very existence has to be the very presence of God in its writing, then we can conclude that we should give it the respect that it deserves. When we decide to respect the Bible is the Holy Inspired Word of God, His written revelation to mankind, we should take heed to it. In order to take heed to the Bible, we must know what it says, and then we need to apply it to our lives. It is really just that simple[2]!"

The Psalmist is so dedicated to keeping God's transforming Word in his life that he takes it a step further and says...

> Psalm 119:10-11 With my whole heart have I sought thee: O let me not wander from thy commandments. Thy word have I hid in mine heart, that I might not sin against thee.

Now there is an attitude that seeks God! He is seeking God with his whole heart and declares his desire not to wander. Wandering from God can only mean one is heading back into the world's thinking, the reprobate mindset. The Psalmist takes it one step further and says he will hide God's Word in his heart; *he is going to memorize it, so he cannot be far from it*. The Psalmist gets it. Apart from God's Word, he is prone to sin, and with God's Word close on his mind inhibiting sin, he is on much safer ground.

I can anticipate someone reasoning that they are capable of memorizing God's Word and at the same time committing sin. Sure we can do that, but that is not taking heed or paying attention to God's Word. That is not capturing the thoughts of God and putting them into play in life. To do that is merely a memory exercise.

On the flip side, when someone is actively and willfully sinning, do you ever notice them quoting Scripture as they do their illegal activities? Do the druggies memorize scripture while they are shooting up? Are people who are embezzling from their companies heeding scripture? No, No, and NO!

Truly, we are all prone to sin but a good solid knowledge can keep you from most of those mistakes. Jesus gave us a Biblical principle statement. As He spoke to the religious elite of the first century, Jesus said...

> Matthew 22:29 Ye do err, not knowing the scriptures, nor the power of God.

If you don't know what God's Word says or understand HIM, Jesus says you make mistakes. Simply throwing this verse into reverse shows us that a good knowledge of Scripture and a solid understanding of God can keep us from these mistakes. Knowing God and His Word will guide us away from error.

I'm going to do something now that most Bible teachers won't do. I'm going to tell you; please, be selfish! Be selfish about getting God's Word into your life and letting it unleash its transforming power to Renew your View. Be selfish to let God's Word create that inside-out change that will change you from the inside-out. Put off the reprobate mindset, renew your mind, and move into the godly mindset. Let us no more be tossed to and fro by every wind of doctrine; let us behave in a Christlike manner.

[1]The Wiersbe Bible Commentary, Warren W Wiersbe, Pg441-442, David C Cook Publishers, Colorado Springs CO

[2]Obvious Choices: Can I Really Believe, Mike VanBruggen, Pg47, Grounded Faith Publications, Sydney Mines NS, Canada

Chapter Four
The Example of the Believers

Back in Michigan when I was little, I wanted to be BIG in the world. I didn't see how anyone could do something that I couldn't eventually do when I grew. I knew I had to practice, but I knew I would be able to do it. Hey, my reasoning was simple. They have two arms, and I have two arms. They have two legs, and I have two legs. They can see what to do, and I can see what to do. I just thought I could do anything. Anything that captured my attention, I would try to do.

Everything that captured my attention was mostly sports and games. I imagined myself playing pro sports, anxiously waiting for my body to grow, so I could do all those things and be on TV. Once when I was little, I slept with my motorcycle helmet on (only once because it gave me a stiff neck). I made motorcycle noises when Dad would shift the car. When I got new riding gloves, I would wear them to watch the motorcycle daredevil jump on TV. After the jump, I would go out and ride! I would practice all my tricks. I was being an example of a motorcycle daredevil.

When I would watch baseball, my renewed mindset would be to go play baseball. I would sleep with my uniform on and my trusty mitt or bat in my hand. When I would watch football, it was the same; throw, catch, kick, tackle. Sleep with a football and a uniform. I just thought if I was going to be a sports star, I had to live the part.

Well, that's the idea I want to carry into this chapter. To be an example of a motorcycle daredevil, I had to look, feel, breathe, and talk the part. It is kind of like that being an authentic Christian who is growing up into the head which is Christ. We have to move toward whatever it is that we want to be an example of, in this case, we want to behave like Christ.

We talked about the renewing of the mind toward maturity in Christlikeness in the last chapter. It is that renewing, an inside-out transformation from the reprobate mindset to the godly mindset, that brings us to the point of being an example of the believers.

I've mentioned a famous motorcycle daredevil as a pattern to follow if you want to be a motorcycle daredevil. The pattern works! Evel Knievel's own son, Robbie, followed in his dad's footsteps and had a pretty good career doing the same kinds of things his dad did. I suppose I could have done that too, but fear and common sense held me back (I could have been a star!).

Now let us look at the patterns for being an example of the believers in Christ. We mentioned the discipler/disciple relationship of the Apostle Paul and young Timothy earlier in this book. Here is what Paul tells Timothy in his letter to him:

> 1 Timothy 4:12 Let no man despise thy youth; <u>but be thou an example of the believers</u>, in word, in conversation, in charity, in spirit, in faith, in purity. (Underline Mine)

Paul tells Timothy to be an example of the believers; a good example is intended. We can tell that from the subsequent list that follows all the way to verse 16. Paul is saying that Timothy should show an "obvious conduct" that would point him out as an example of the believers. Paul believes Timothy can really behave this way, and I believe we can too. Before we get into the list that follows the phrase 'example of the believers' in v12, let's spend some time looking at the phrase itself.

There are good examples and bad examples in the Bible. We are going to focus on a few of the more helpful and good examples that will point us toward the spiritual growth we are looking for. We will look at five instances of good and godly examples before we come back to expand on 1 Timothy 4:12.

The Example of the Believers is a Servant...

Let us point out that Jesus left us a lifetime of good examples; overall through the life and ministry of Jesus Christ He gave us the example of servanthood. Jesus even says "I have given you an example". The setting is this; on the night Jesus was betrayed he had dinner with his disciples. We call this event 'The Last Supper'. Jesus got up from supper and washed the feet of the men He was serving alongside of.

The idea goes forward that if you're Lord and Master can serve you, then you can serve others. Let's see the passage.

> John 13:14-15 If I then, your Lord and Master, have washed your feet; ye also ought to wash one another's feet. For <u>I have given you an example, that ye should do as I have done to you</u>. (Underline Mine)

Jesus is the Lord and Master; no one questions who the leader is when Jesus is around. Yet Jesus sets an example of service and humility. The God of the universe put on a towel and bent over the feet of those He loved and washed the smelly road waste away. The Lord and Master became the servant. He did what He needed to do to meet their need.

The Example of the Believers is Humble...

Jesus shows us humility in the service He rendered. There was no news coverage like today. Jesus' polling numbers did not climb with every scrubbing motion of His hand. No, He was showing a pattern of humble servanthood from a caring and loving heart. Jesus had nothing to personally gain from His foot washing exercise. Jesus was giving them (and us) a lesson to use as we serve Him. This is really the base attitude for the example of the believers, service from a pure heart of concern for others in the name of Christ.

Jesus was not only giving us an example to follow, He was living the example as well. Just hours after Jesus washed the feet of His disciples, He was betrayed with a kiss and led off to slaughter. Paul captures the thought we are looking for in one of his epistles.

> Philippians 2:5-8 Let this mind be in you, which was also in Christ Jesus: Who, being in the form of God, thought it not robbery to be equal with God: But made himself of no reputation, and took upon him the form of a servant, and was made in the likeness of men: And being found in fashion as a man, he humbled himself, and became obedient unto death, even the death of the cross. (Underline Mine)

Let this mind be in you... which mind? The reprobate mind? No! The godly mind or the Christlike mind. That's what mind Paul suggests should be in you. It is the attitude that Christ carried to the cross, humbly serving us. Jesus stepping away from His lofty attributes of godliness to become like us, equal with God but found in fashion as a man. Humbled and empty, obedient to do what was needed to wash, not our feet, but our sins away from us. It took His death as a man to pay the penalty for our sins, and it took His rising again on the third day, so we can live with Him.

What do you think hurt more: the beating and nailing to the cross or the hours of separation from God on the cross and the shame of dying a criminal's death? I can't answer that question, but I can say this; none of it was pleasant. Washing the disciples' feet was easy compared to dying on the cross. This is truly the ultimate display of humble service from a caring and loving God who bowed low to save us. This is our example of attitude.

The Example of the Believers Suffers for their Faith...

Peter equates being an example of the believers with following Christ in His sufferings. We deserve our sufferings because of our sin; it is not noble to suffer when you deserve it. Jesus had no sin and therefore deserved no suffering. Yet Jesus suffered more than we ever will. If we are humbly serving God, ministering, and bringing people closer to God through Christ, and we suffer, it is worth thanks. That attitude honors God because it follows after Christ's example.

> 1 Peter 2:19-21 For this is thankworthy, if a man for conscience toward God endure grief, suffering wrongfully. For what glory is it, if, when ye be buffeted for your faults, ye shall take it patiently? but if, when ye do well, and suffer for it, ye take it patiently, this is acceptable with God. <u>For even hereunto were ye called: because Christ also suffered for us, leaving us an example, that ye should follow his steps </u>(Underline Mine)

Again, we see that Christ suffering is leaving an example for us. See the last line; we were called into His sufferings. Okay. We are not all called to die on a cross, but we are all called to selflessly serve others for the sake of Christ. It is tough to serve. People take up our time and energy. People slow down our progress. People have difficult problems.

We suffer when they suffer, and we suffer trying to care for them.

Unrelenting service in the face of ridicule is hard to take unless you have the mind of Christ. Jesus is the humble servant who met people where their need was and helped bring them to where He was. James gives us an interesting perspective on this mindset of facing trials.

> James 1:2-4 My brethren, count it all joy when ye fall into divers temptations; Knowing this, that the trying of your faith worketh patience. But let patience have her perfect work, that ye may be perfect and entire, wanting nothing.

We should be happy when we face these trials in life as servants of the Lord because of the benefits we will receive. The trial of our faith in Christ brings about patience in our faith which is strength and resilience. The perfect work of that patience, or the byproduct of that strong faith, is maturity. Remember that we don't want to be like children being blown around by every wind of doctrine. We want to grow to maturity. This is part of the process!

Joyfully serve with the humble mindset of Christ and happily join with the sufferings He endured. You may never have to wash anyone's feet, but you should be willing to. It glorifies God when you put others before yourself. To be an example of the believers is to follow the example of Christ which includes suffering.

The Example of the Believers is Determined...

In Thessalonica, the believers within the new church that Paul started there saw an example of the believers then became examples of the believers. As the Gospel was being introduced in Thessalonica, there was plenty of opposition and danger. We could use the word 'sufferings'. Paul and Silas came with Timothy to Thessalonica, where they reasoned with those who met in the synagogue. Paul and his group had good success there until some jealous Jewish worshippers became harmful. Paul and Silas were forced to leave quickly.

However, in as little as three weeks, the Christian church in Thessalonica started. Sufferings were normal for them. They had received the Word being young in their faith and suffered persecution simultaneously. They had assurance from the Holy Spirit that they were on the right track, and they stayed the course. Here is the passage...

> 1 Thessalonians 1:5-7 For our gospel came not unto you in word only, but also in power, and in the Holy Ghost, and in much assurance; as ye know what manner of men we were among you for your sake. And ye became followers of us, and of the Lord, having received the word in much affliction, with joy of the Holy Ghost: So that ye were ensamples to all that believe in Macedonia and Achaia. (Underline Mine)

In the middle of that passage, Paul says, "...ye know what manner of men we were among you". You know that we are sincere about our conviction of Jesus Christ. You know that we are respectful and honest. You know because you have seen us personally, and you have gone eyeball to eyeball with us.

Then Paul says, "And ye became followers of us and of the Lord". We were an example of godliness to you, and in following us, you came closer to God. That is discipleship! That is an example of the believers and is what the believers in Thessalonica would emulate. Finally, later in the verse, Paul tells them that they became the examples to all the believers in the region where they lived. Their example was born in sufferings, and their conduct within those sufferings excelled as the example.

Paul goes onto talk about examples again to the Thessalonian believers. It is a manner of conduct.

> 2 Thessalonians 3:7-9 For yourselves know how ye ought to follow us: for we behaved not ourselves disorderly among you; Neither did we eat any man's bread for naught; but wrought with labor and travail night and day, that we might not be chargeable to any of you: Not because we have not power, <u>but to make ourselves an ensample unto you to follow us</u>. (Underline Mine)

Paul and the men had the right to receive housing and food in return for their service to the church. They chose rather to work harder, laboring day and night and earning their living, not taking anything from anyone. Paul, Silas, and Timothy chose to take the harder route for the benefit of these young believers. What is the reason they wanted to do the extra work? Paul and the group didn't want to be a stumbling block to their spiritual growth; they wanted to be examples to follow.

Hard work is one of those things we are called to do. It is part of love and respect; we pull our weight in society. The result of hard work is that we can approach unbelievers with a clean slate, not wanting anything from them because we have earned everything we need.

> 1 Thessalonians 4:9-12 But as touching brotherly love ye need not that I write unto you: for ye yourselves are taught of God to love one another. And indeed ye do it toward all the brethren which are in all Macedonia: but we beseech you, brethren, that ye increase more and more; And that ye study to be quiet, and to do your own business, and to work with your own hands, as we commanded you; That ye may walk honestly toward them that are without, and that ye may have lack of nothing. (Underline Mine)

Paul did not have to teach them again to take care of one another, but he encourages them as examples to do their work, so they can have opportunity to bless others. One avenue of blessing would be that they have their own resources to go and help someone without cost. Another avenue of blessing would be that they can afford to supply some of the need to those they reach out to. Still another avenue of blessing is that they are known as reliable and productive members of society. Their reputation is untarnished. That's just as much a part of the example as the Gospel itself.

The Example of the Believers is Blameless...

Paul talks to Titus about this very thing although he does not use the word 'example' in the passage. It is clear that Paul considers an untarnished reputation a valuable quality in the example of the believers.

> Titus 2:7-8 In all things <u>shewing thyself a pattern of good works</u>: in doctrine shewing uncorruptness, gravity, sincerity, sound speech, <u>that cannot be condemned</u>; that he that is of the contrary part may be ashamed, <u>having no evil thing to say of you</u>. (Underline Mine)

This is why Paul behaved as he did in Thessalonica (and we can assume this behavioral pattern was normal for him). He did this to establish a pattern of good works, so that condemnation cannot occur, and no evil thing can be said. Everything Paul represented was read into his message. If he was a slouch as a representative of Christ, it reflected on Christ. Paul says an example of the believers reflects favorably upon Jesus and not as a reproach upon Him.

The pattern of good works that reflect favorably upon Christ includes true doctrine, a serious approach, steadfast belief, and good speech. Part of the suffering of a close walk with the Lord is that everyone is watching and waiting for you to mess up. It can mean a lot of pressure, but it doesn't have to. You have the choice to consider it all joy and have your faith matured by those stresses. It is an attitude shift caused by the renewing of the mind that we talked about earlier.

Chapter Five
Use Your Indicators

From Chapter 4 we saw five characteristics to be desired in being an example of the believers...

The Example of the Believers is a Servant...

The Example of the Believers is Humble...

The Example of the Believers Suffers for their Faith...

The Example of the Believers is Determined...

The Example of the Believers is Blameless...

Now, we have to realize that every aspect of our lives needs to show these qualities in each area and activity. As we begin to see what an example of the believers is, we begin to notice another quality that a true example of the believers becomes.

The Example of the Believer Becomes Obvious...

Obvious because of the behavior they sustain. Obvious because of the stability they maintain. They are obvious because the application of God's Word to their lives changes them into something different from the world, and the worldly life that is common today.

When I grew to be a young adult, I began to ride street motorcycles. I had a nice maroon Yamaha 550 Maxim. Like all road bikes it had turn signals on it and 4 way flashers. There was an indicator that showed me when my high beams were on, and there was an indicator that showed me if my oil was low. Some of the indicators could be seen by other drivers, so they would know my next intention. Other indicators helped me to know what was going on with the inner workings of the motorcycle. I could see there was a problem and make corrections before damage took place in the engine.

The turn signals indicated to other drivers that my obvious intent was to turn in a certain direction. The hazard flashers indicated to other drivers that I was obviously stopped, or there was some road hazard to watch for. The high beam indicator light made it obvious that my high beams were on even if it was not obvious from the light emanating from the front. The oil level indicator sought to be an obvious warning against loss of lubrication in the engine. All these external indicators can give us insight about what is going on within the operation of that motorcycle.

So as with the example of the believer, the indicators are meant to be obvious so that no one looks down upon him because of his age. The Greek word that brings us to the thought of Timothy's youth indicates that he is forty years old or less. It is not like we think of youth today. Still, young people of any age can be respected and respectful if they do what Paul tells Timothy to do. Paul tells Timothy to be obvious in six areas.

> 1 Timothy 4:12 Let no man despise (look down
> upon) thy youth; but be thou an example of the
> believers, in word, in conversation, in charity, in
> spirit, in faith, in purity. (Parenthesis mine)

Be clear, Timothy; let these indicators show others of your inner workings. Let these indicators be seen by others, so they would know your next intention. Let these indicators show others of your maturity both spiritually and socially, of your reliability and of your integrity. Like the tip of an iceberg shows what is beneath the surface in the water, these indicators can show what is beneath the surface in your heart.

It is true that Timothy was a young pastor in the church at Ephesus, and most of us are not pastors, and we do want our pastors to be set apart unto God, but Paul's message to Timothy is also for us. With that thought safely in mind, let's recognize it is also true that the Lord has called each of us to live a life that honors Him. We are called by His name.

Peter talks about this as he writes to believers who are scattered throughout the Roman Empire, most of whom were not pastors...

> 1 Peter 1:15-16 But as he which hath called you is
> holy, so be ye holy in all manner of conversation;
> because it is written, be ye holy; for I am holy.

Peter is quoting the Old Testament book of Leviticus[1] where the Lord God was addressing the Israelites in general, not only the priests. This sanctified or set apart way of life is not for full time Christian service workers only. This lifestyle is for all believers.

An Example in Word

The first indicator has to do with being an example in the words we choose and use. The words that come out of our mouths indicate to others what is in our hearts. They tell what our thoughts and motives are even when we are trying to cover it up, and they communicate who or what we are following. There is definitely a godly speech pattern that emerges as one becomes an example of the believers.

First of all, a godly speech pattern would omit lying.

> Ephesians 4:15 But speaking the truth in love, may grow up into him in all things, which is the head, even Christ:

> Ephesians 4:25 Wherefore putting away lying, speak every man truth with his neighbor: for we are members one of another.

We are talking about sincere communication that would show our maturity as we grow into Christlikeness. We should be speaking the truth with others conveying an element of love and caring for the hearer. Even when we have to bring a hard truth we do it from a heart of compassion. Our purpose in communication is improvement and the building up of each other.

> Ephesians 4:29 Let no corrupt communication proceed out of your mouth, but that which is good to the use of edifying, that it may minister grace unto the hearers.

Corrupt communication and evil, dirty, destructive talk can only serve to tear down those to whom it is aimed. There is no place in the example of the believers for this kind of communication. Can I say this quickly? Coarse jesting and joke telling may be funny for some, but for the person whose expense the joke is, it may be bullying. Fun is only fun when everyone really thinks it is fun, and if someone is angered or hurt by your joke or satirical reference, then you shouldn't have said it.

This is difficult because usually you don't know until the damage is done. When you have offended, even if it was unintentionally, proper communication needs to be used. A sincere apology is in order and is expected from a heart of compassion, humility, and sorrow. Everyone steps over this 'line of speech that tears down' from time to time, but sadly, many of us never make an attempt to step back with a genuinely sincere apology. Rather than focus on what not to say, focus on speech that is edifying and that ministers grace to the hearers!

> Colossians 4:6 Let your speech be always with grace, seasoned with salt, that ye may know how ye ought to answer every man.

Graceful speech or speech with grace includes an element of refinement, a disciplined sort of order to communication. In this case, it is a proper refinement in technical and spiritual terms. There is nothing wrong with speaking a little slang here and there during a casual conversation, but when the conversation turns proper and spiritual we should be able to rise to the level and seriousness of the conversation. No one is saying 'speak perfectly or don't speak at all'; rather what I am suggesting here is that we are able to accomplish communication at the appropriate level to give us credibility as examples of the believers.

The Apostle Paul writes that our speech be seasoned with salt. On the surface, that doesn't make much sense, but back in Paul's day, salt was a preservative. So now we can think of speech that is grace filled and has the action of a preservative. This is speech that delays decay. It is speech that neutralizes the effects of the worldly ideas we become accustomed to. We are talking about speech that produces a lasting effect for the good of the hearer rather than the rottenness that comes by worldly chatter.

In Colossians 4:6, and in another verse in 1 Peter, we are instructed to know how to answer or speak to anyone.

> 1 Peter 3:15 But sanctify the Lord God in your hearts: and be ready always to give an answer to every man that asketh you a reason of the hope that is in you with meekness and fear:

This communication of telling another of the hope that is in us as believers will have to include all the principles of good and godly speech. First of all, don't ignore that we need to sanctify or set apart ourselves to the Lord in our hearts before we begin to talk. This idea includes all areas of our lives; these things are all inter-connected. If we talk a good game and say all the right things, but our actions don't measure up to our talking points, then our talk is cheap.

Godly speech comes from a godly life. We can easily see that a godly life is a life that is ready to answer every man that asks about the hope that is in them, (and that hope is our salvation in Jesus Christ).

An Example in Conduct

The next indicator is our conduct or behavior. The word in 1 Timothy 4:12 and the word in the verse I am about to share is 'conversation' which is an old English way of discussing 'conduct' or 'behavior'.

> Philippians 1:27a Only let your conversation (conduct or behavior) be as it becometh the gospel of Christ: (Parenthesis mine)

Our conduct as examples of the believers is very important, as we just said. If our walk and our talk don't measure up, we will be seen as a phony. We need to show by our behavior that our lives are being guided by the Word of God.

> Titus 2:7-8 In all things shewing thyself a pattern of good works: in doctrine shewing un-corruptness, gravity, sincerity, Sound speech, that cannot be

condemned; that he that is of the contrary part may be ashamed, having no evil thing to say of you.

Believers need to show a pattern of good and not contradictory works. A pattern of things we do that makes sense when one considers that we call ourselves Christian. This would resemble a genuine seriousness that cannot be doomed to failure or judged as inadequate by an unbeliever. In other words, what we do has to complement what we say, and both our words and conduct have to be as it becomes the Gospel message of Christ. All of this verbal and non-verbal communication must be Christlike in nature.

Someone who had this indicator was Daniel from the book of Daniel in the Bible. We can really see this godly behavior pattern throughout his life.

> Daniel 1:8a But Daniel purposed in his heart that he would not defile himself with the portion of the king's meat, nor with the wine which he drank: therefore he requested of the prince of the eunuchs that he might not defile himself.

Daniel was really taking a chance with his physical wellbeing by refusing the king's food. Daniel knew that the king's food had been sacrificed to idols and eating it would be an offense to God and would be seen as a concession to the Babylonian false gods. He would rather be executed than behave in a way that would defile the God of Heaven. Daniel purposed in his heart and followed that purpose.

Much later in his life, Daniel was the target of a plot. There was a conspiracy against him. The ungodly governors of Babylon wanted to get rid of Daniel, but as they investigated his long life, they could find no fault against him. Could any of us endure an investigation like that and come out clean? Daniel did. Here is the passage that describes what happened...

> Daniel 6:4-5 Then the presidents and princes sought to find occasion against Daniel concerning the kingdom; but they could find none occasion nor fault; forasmuch as he was faithful, neither was there any error or fault found in him. Then said these men, we shall not find any occasion against this Daniel, except we find it against him concerning the law of his God.

The only way they could find to trip up Daniel was to make a law that contradicted Daniel's practice concerning his God. They knew Daniel's character and behavior. His indicators were on, and he would not forsake his God. In the following verses, they were able to convince King Darius to make a new law that anyone who asks petition of any god or man other than King Darius for the next 30 days would be in violation and be thrown into the lion's den.

The end result of this law would be that if Daniel were caught praying to God, he would be guilty and punished by being thrown into the lion's den. What did Daniel do when he knew this law was going into effect? He went home to pray about it.

Daniel 6:10 Now when Daniel knew that the writing was signed, he went into his house; and his windows being open in his chamber toward Jerusalem, he kneeled upon his knees three times a day, and prayed, and gave thanks before his God, as he did aforetime.

Daniel's godly behavior and his example to the believers (and non-believers) was so strong and consistent that they could use it against him. That is a testimony of a man without hypocrisy. This plan would not work on many Christians today due to the chameleon effect. The "chameleon effect" is seen in Christianity that reflects the world we live in rather than the God that gave us this life.

A Hypocritical Chameleon Effect Christianity is what Paul warned Titus about.

Titus 1:15-16 Unto the pure all things are pure: but unto them that are defiled and unbelieving is nothing pure; but even their mind and conscience is defiled. They profess that they know God; but in works they deny him, being abominable, and disobedient, and unto every good work reprobate.

To those who are pure and assume the best from others, some activities may seem acceptable, but Paul indicates here that the ungodly might not see things in such a forgiving way. Please just know that evil people see situations completely differently than the righteous. The righteous would see a cashier walking away from an open till as an opportunity to help them and protect that money until they come back. The evil person would immediately see an opportunity for theft. In that same way, the ungodly sees sin opportunities in situations that we don't consider because we don't think like that. So in that line of thought, we as the examples of the believers have to consider how others see the things we are doing.

Peter sums it up nicely.

> 1 Peter 2:12 Having your conversation (Conduct or Behavior) honest among the Gentiles (World System): that, whereas they speak against you as evildoers, they may by your good works, which they shall behold, glorify God in the day of visitation. (Parenthesis mine)

The example of the believers behaves honestly and uprightly in this world and its worldly system glorifying God. It is the behavior they see that gives them cause to look into this God that we follow and that brings glory to God!

An Example in Love

The third indicator on our list is love or charity. As we get into this little section, let me explain some words, so we don't get confused in our discussion. As we are working through the indicator words of 1 Timothy 4:12, the word that is translated 'love' from the original Greek is agape. Here is one definition of agape love: **Agape** (Ancient Greek:

ἀγάπη, agápē) is "love: the highest form of love, unconditional love; the love of God for man and of man for God."

Forms of the same Greek word, also seen as Agape Love, can be translated as 'charity'. The entire thought here is that of someone who loves unconditionally and will go to any length to aid or assist another without promise of any benefit to the one who is doing the loving. It is a selfless care for someone else. We can see then how the translators might have chosen the English word 'love' at times while at other times they might have settled on the word 'charity'.

Here is the ultimate example of this charitable love...

> Romans 5:6-8 For when we were yet without strength, in due time Christ died for the ungodly. For scarcely for a righteous man will one die: yet peradventure for a good man some would even dare to die. But God commendeth (demonstrated) his love toward us, in that, while we were yet sinners, Christ died for us. (Parenthesis mine)

God loves people; we know that from one of the most famous verses of the Bible, John 3:16 – "For God so loved the world". Christ the Example died for us, loving us when we deserved no love. From that unlimited and unconditional love, Christ compels us to love also. We need to love the unlovable sinners from outside the church, those who are not in our comfortable circle of Christian friends.

Some of the religious elite of Israel were gathered one day, and one of them asked Jesus a question. It wasn't really an innocent question so that the man might learn; it was a manipulative question designed to put Jesus into a no-win situation.

> Matthew 22:35-36 Then one of them, which was a lawyer, asked him a question, tempting him, and saying, Master, which is the great commandment in the law?

The question is trying to point Jesus towards a performance based Christianity, what is the biggest and best rule to keep? Jesus would not be fooled; His answer redirects the question towards a relationship based Christianity. The love of God focused toward mankind with the result of the love of mankind focused back on God.

> Matthew 22:37-39 Jesus said unto him, Thou shalt love the Lord thy God with all thy heart, and with all thy soul, and with all thy mind. This is the first and great commandment. And the second is like unto it, Thou shalt love thy neighbor as thyself.

If you have to live by rules here are two rules to live by: love God so much that you would never do anything wrong, and love others like you love yourself, so you will never do anything harmful to them either. In fact, Jesus goes on to say in verse 40 that every other guideline, commandment, and ideal in Scripture depends on this kind of love.

In Jesus, we see the example of someone so close to God that He willingly intercedes for people of all shapes and sizes because it is the will of the Father. Jesus loved his disciples in a personal way, caring about their needs and teaching them godliness, preparing them for future ministry. Then for those of us who hear of Him through the ministry of others, His love shines through because He has made the sacrifice for us. Through this Love, God forgives when we accept and trust Him.

God is not calling us to die for another; He has completed that work. God is calling us to be an example of the believers by demonstrating love for people as HE has.

> 1 Peter 4:8 And above all things have fervent charity among yourselves: for charity shall cover the multitude of sins.

Dr. David Jeremiah comments on this verse saying, "Peter places the highest priority on loving one another. Fervent love that openly reaches out and lovingly goes the extra distance is what makes Christians shine as lights to a dark world... God's people should not seek to reveal or dwell on anyone's past sins; rather they should be quick to forgive and unwilling to hold others faults against them."[2]

As the example of the believers acts on Jesus' words to love God with everything and love others as yourself, it shows as a forgiving and forbearing servant that wants the best for the other party. Peter's comment here reflects an old proverb...

> Proverbs 10:12 Hatred stirreth up strifes: but love covereth all sins.

Love forgives but hatred causes trouble. We see the Apostle Paul write about the power of the love of God as it flows through us. In 1 Corinthians 13:1-3, Paul effectively says that without love, every other thing is useless. Love is the power behind the action and because it is love the power is for the good and not for the bad. Because of the love of God that we emulate, we can minister to others.

> 1 Corinthians 13:4-8a Charity suffereth long, and is kind; charity envieth not; charity vaunteth (does not brag) not itself, is not puffed up, Doth not behave itself unseemly, seeketh not her own, is not easily provoked, thinketh no evil; Rejoiceth not in iniquity, but rejoiceth in the truth; Beareth all things, believeth all things, hopeth all things, endureth all things. Charity never faileth... (Parenthesis mine)

The love of God never fails us and if we properly reflect that godly love to others, it will not fail to show us as examples of the believers.

An Example in Spirit

To be an example of the believers in spirit seems to look like a combination of proper conduct combined with proper motivation like love and charity sprinkled with fervent or enthusiastic participation. This shows a willingness to be in Christ, to be submissive to the things of Christ to produce Christlikeness in one's life. We are not talking about agreeing to a list of do's and don'ts but a willful attitude of staying inside the guidelines for the purpose of bringing forth godly fruit in our lives. Abiding or living in the way of Christ and allowing Him to abide and live with us.

> John 15:4-5 Abide in me, and I in you. As the branch cannot bear fruit of itself, except it abide in the vine; no more can ye, except ye abide in me. I am the vine, ye are the branches: He that abideth in me, and I in him, the same bringeth forth much fruit: for without me ye can do nothing.

In this analogy Jesus is describing a vine that has had a branch grafted in, that means a branch attached to a vine. The branch is then dependent on the vine for its moisture and nourishment through the root system of the vine. The vine supplies for the branch, and the branch brings fruit for the vine. The branch must however take the nutrients the vine provides staying within the context of the vine. Without the vine, the branch would die. If the branch is loosely connected, it cannot get the proper nutrition and will not thrive.

Together, the vine and the branch can produce much fruit. Over time, the connection at the graft will become tighter and tighter making the nutrition transfer more and more secure. The vine and the branch will grow together and become inseparable, yet the branch will always be dependent on the vine for its sustenance.

The proper spirit of the example of the believer is to be that willing branch that is grafted into the vine – Jesus Christ. We must be willingly and enthusiastically living and growing by God's word. We must let the Lord bring forth whatever fruit He desires from our lives. It is a willingness to be an authentic, practicing believer that lives and abides in Christ.

An Example in Faith

Next, we are to have the indicator of faith. To be an example of the believers means we must have first had some faith. If we didn't have faith, we wouldn't be called believers in Jesus Christ; we wouldn't have trusted Him with our eternal welfare and wellbeing. Being a believer by definition means we are examples of faith. Here is a very familiar passage that says it very simply.

> Ephesians 2:8-9 For by grace are ye saved through faith; and that not of yourselves: it is the gift of God: Not of works, lest any man should boast.

Okay, so we are saved by the grace of God through faith in Him, but the term faith can be a bit vague. Synonyms for faith include words like trust, reliance, confidence, belief, and conviction. It is a trust in God to complete His promise to us of salvation through that simple faith. There is a good definition of faith within the context of Scripture that we should see.

> Hebrews 11:1 Now faith is the substance of things hoped for, the evidence of things not seen.

The thing that seems like it is something we can cling to, the substance of that vague yet specific promise is our faith or belief or trust in God. We have to believe that God is who He says He is and that He will do what He says He will do. The evidence is in the things we have not seen yet but have seen evidence of. For example, if you have read my first book, Obvious Choices, I took a lot of time there to explain many evidences that the Bible as we have it cannot exist apart from God. There has to be a supreme being out there who superintended the production of the 66 books that were written by some 40 authors over a time period of about 1500 years. They were originally written in three languages from different regions of the world, yet perfectly coincided into one perfect message to us.

We can see the evidence, so we can conclude there is a God behind it. Therefore, we can believe or have faith in that God. Because that faith or belief has a reason behind it, that faith has substance to cling to. When I say 'cling', I don't mean an act of desperation. I am using the word 'cling' in a sense like 'adhere or stick to' indicating a holding on that will not be released. It will not be released because the faith is strong.

We need faith to please God!

> Hebrews 11:6 But without faith it is impossible to please him: for he that cometh to God must believe that he is, and that he is a rewarder of them that diligently seek him.

Our faith pleases Him because we believe Him, that He is there and that He wants to be active with us. God wants us to seek Him and follow after His ways!

> 1 Timothy 6:11-12 But thou, O man of God, flee these things; and follow after righteousness, godliness, faith, love, patience, meekness. Fight the good fight of faith, lay hold on eternal life, whereunto thou art also called, and hast professed a good profession before many witnesses.

Note the two applications of faith in these verses. Faith is listed as something to be pursued along with righteousness, godliness, love, patience, and meekness. These are all similar to the things we have been talking about. It is all part of a process of being engrafted as a branch into the master vine. We believe God, so we learn more about Him. Learning more about Him causes us to believe God more which in turn causes us to learn more about Him. This process goes on and on. It could be the paragraph that never ends! I'll let your imagination take it as far as you want while I go on to my next point.

There is a good fight of faith mentioned. This is the struggle we incur when we profess the Lord, and the world begins to oppose us. Sometimes we overtly take direct opposition to our own faith in the Lord, and sometimes it happens covertly, when the opposition seeks to undermine us and our faith in God. Whether it is a direct assault or a sneak attack, the idea here is that we battle for our faith. The Greek word that comes across as 'fight' is more literally translated as 'agonize'. Certainly if we are in a fight we agonize, so you can see how fight or struggle would apply, but to fill out the feeling of the passage, it is hardship; it is agony.

The Apostle Paul gives us some insight as to what the look of this 'fight of faith' is like in a mature Christian whose days on earth are nearly done. Paul reflects on his life as a Christian and says...

> 2 Timothy 4:7 I have fought a good fight, I have finished my course, I have kept the faith

Paul sees that he contended well for the faith. He has run his course, and he has been an example of the believers in faith. Through all the difficulties and persecutions that came his way, he never quit believing, never quit trusting, and he never quit contending for God. God didn't give up on Paul. Now will He give up on us? An example of the believers lives it out by not quitting on God.

An Example in Purity

The indicator of purity may be called the maintenance man of all the indicators. Purity reflects holiness which demonstrates the indicators in ultimate fullness. It is the manifestation of all the indicators in one while pushing each to its fullest extent.

Many well intentioned pastors, youth pastors, and youth leaders take the word 'purity' and immediately jump to sexual sins giving the students a heavy dose of do's and don'ts -- mostly don'ts. Surely there are issues there to be dealt with, and we should call them what they are rather than use 'purity' as some kind of code word. I've even heard 'purity' talks that never mentioned God or the Bible.

There are many ways to be impure that don't have anything to do with sex or sexuality. Youth are active in improper ways all over the world. I hope we can agree that a list of *Thou Shalt Not's* won't really address the problems we face. While we are at it, maybe we could admit that people of all ages and both genders are involved in sexual sins. The problem is not age related, it is sin related.

As a pastor in Ephesus, Timothy undoubtedly faced many tests in the area of these kinds of sins. Ephesus was an industry leader in sexual sin, sensuality, and temptation. The key to Timothy's victory over the temptations he might have faced was not found in staying out of certain districts of the city or walking on a certain side of the street. The victory for this battle began in his mind, supported in his relationship with his discipler, Paul, and ultimately defined in his relationship with God.

It will be helpful to remember Chapter Three: Renew Your View. In that chapter, we talked about the reprobate mindset being transformed from the inside out to a godly mindset. One key passages out of the many we sought there was from Psalm 119.

> Psalms 119:9-12 Wherewithal shall a young man cleanse his way? by taking heed thereto according to thy word. With my whole heart have I sought thee: O let me not wander from thy commandments. Thy word have I hid in mine heart, that I might not sin against thee. Blessed art thou, O LORD: teach me thy statutes.

A clean mind, with a godly outlook, built from a sincere relationship with God and His Word is the foundation for purity. Purity in its core is not what we do and don't do with our body. It is what we do and don't do in our mind. It all starts there. This verse says to cleanse our actions we must learn and apply God's Word to our lives.

The battle of the brain manifests itself in the actions of our bodies, our organizations, and our governments. The same can be said for each of our indicators of the examples of the believers. Impurities in our thoughts will produce impure speech, impure behavior, impure attitudes, an impure faith (if there is faith at all), and an impure walk. This idea of purity, or impurity, only having to do with sexual sin is a mono-focus that ignores the display of thousands of wrongs (impurities) that are being done in increasing numbers everywhere we look.

The reverse of this world driven by impurity could look something like this...

> Philippians 4:8 Finally, brethren, whatsoever things are true, whatsoever things are honest, whatsoever things are just, whatsoever things are pure, whatsoever things are lovely, whatsoever things are of good report; if there be any virtue, and if there be any praise, think on these things.

It is a godliness that sticks to the Word of God, gains its attitudes from the knowledge of God, and focuses on things that are compatible with godliness. You see that words like true, honest, just (righteous), and pure all lead you to the same source which is God. You can go on with things that are lovely, of good report (wholesome), virtuous, and praise worthy; think on all of these things. As we meditate on good things of God, we come to the next verse.

> Philippians 4:9 Those things, which ye have both learned, and received, and heard, and seen in me, do: and the God of peace shall be with you.

Paul says those things there in that list and the other godly things which I taught you, do them. Starting from your brain and showing through to your body, do those things, and the God of Peace will be with you. God is all about purity, but it doesn't start with the external you; it begins with a renewed view in the internal you.

Here is the idea from another viewpoint, check out this verse;

> 1 Thessalonians 5:22-23 Abstain from all appearance of evil. And the very God of peace sanctify you wholly; and I pray God your whole spirit and soul and body be preserved blameless unto the coming of our Lord Jesus Christ.

Stay away from all appearance of evil. Let it not even be said that you were thinking about doing something sinful because you stayed away from the venue of evil. Get away from those situations and let God work in your life! He will sanctify you. Going back to the Greek again, the word that is translated 'sanctified' is the Greek root word for 'holy'. Sanctification is a progressive process whereby we become more holy as we come closer and closer to godliness.

If we are being successfully sanctified (in other words we are not blocking the process of God bringing us closer to HIM), we are living closer and closer to God. So close to God that we would not violate His will for our lives. Our behavior would reflect that closeness even if it looks like we might have an opportunity to violate His trust. Just because we might be able to get away with something the mere opportunity would not open the door for us to misbehave, we value the process of living closer and closer to God more than we value the fleeting pleasures of sin.

Purity says... I don't have a thought of impropriety because my thoughts are only on godliness. My thoughts are only on godliness so my body is focused on godliness. Because my body and my mind are focused on godliness there is no room for worldliness or impurity. Purity is not about the setting we find ourselves in or the culture we live in; purity is about holiness and holiness is about godliness.

[1]Leviticus 11:44, 19:2, and 20:7

[2]Dr David Jeremiah, 2013, The Jeremiah Study Bible, Pg. 1790 notes, Worthy Publishing

Chapter Six
Practice Indicates Progress

By the time I was in my early forties my wife and I had three children, and we all loved to ride bikes. At the time we were making decent money, and I had purchased each one in the family their own 21 speed mountain bike. We would love to go camping in this particular state park where there were trails to ride. This park had everything from easy trails for the beginners to difficult trails for the very experienced riders.

When we started, all we could do the easy trail. So we began to work our way up through the different trails until we were trying the most demanding. We would go out and try. We might succeed, or we might fail; but we always had fun. We would relive the events of the rides each night telling story after story around the campfire. Some of the things that happened out there many years ago still come up in family stories.

There was a sand pit there that we had a lot of trouble getting through. We would lose balance and fall, or we would get bogged down in the sand. Then one day one of us got through it. The secret was to be committed 100% to charging through the sand, adjusting to the proper gear, and peddling hard; no matter what. That sand pit was a challenge, difficult enough that it was never a certainty that we would get through. We became skilled enough that we could navigate that sand pit almost every time.

Every once in a while we would take some guests with us to ride on these trails. Each time we did, we were quickly reminded that our friends had not practiced; they had not thought about things like sand pits. What we found out was that our discussion and practice of the bike riding principles gave us great progress against those obstacles. Even though our friends knew how to ride a bike, they did not know how to navigate the hazards on the trail.

We were devoted to the idea of doing everything we could to succeed. That's the same kind of devotion we need to develop spiritually, so we don't get stuck in the sand pits of life. That's what Paul the discipler tells Timothy the disciple in the last verses of 1 Timothy 4.

> 1 Timothy 4:15 Meditate upon these things; give thyself wholly to them; that thy profiting may appear to all.

Taking God's Word to heart, thinking it through, and being committed to work hard at it through every trial and hazard gives us progress or profiting against those hazards. The sand pits of life are out there, but they don't have to stop us.

Pastor Warren Wiersbe picks this phrase "that thy profiting may appear to all"[1] as the key thought of this section of the book. When we are considering disciples and those that disciple them, it seems obvious that we should be able to see the progress we are making. In fact, we would see people on the bike trails asking others how they handled a particular section, the reasoning is simple... if you want to know how to do something, find someone who is already doing it then ask them how. So if you want to grow spiritually, find out how from someone who is obviously growing closer to God.

Now remember the verse, meditate and give yourself wholly to the process. We have to go beyond mere learning and get into the area of participation. Practice those indicators from v12 that thy profiting may appear to all.

Be An Example in Word

Be An Example in Conduct

Be An Example in Love

Be An Example in Spirit

Be An Example in Faith

Be An Example in Purity

Let everyone see us peddling hard and let it be known that we are shifting through the gears and the momentum is building. Make it so all can see that progress is being made, and progress is amplified by being 'all in', given wholly to those indicators you're meditating on.

1 Timothy 4:13 Till I come, give attendance to reading, to exhortation, to doctrine.

Give attendance to or put an emphasis on the reading of God's Word. Use the thing that tunes us to God to tune us to God. What else would you use it for? Too often people get caught up in religion doing good deeds and neglect the thing that took them to that service in the first place. Each one of our indicators of the example of the believers is grounded in the Word of God. Doesn't it make common sense then to stay grounded in God's Word? Paul thought so!

Stay close to God's Word and encourage others to do the same.

> 2 Timothy 2:15 Study to shew thyself approved unto God, a workman that needeth not to be ashamed, rightly dividing the word of truth.

Note the first word, 'study'. God approves of our studying His Word. If we are going to be a witness, be a disciple, or have a disciple, knowing and handling God's Word correctly is essential. We have to give attention to the reading of the Word of God.

Now, it is true that Timothy was a pastor and it is obvious that pastors have to study God's Word. You might be thinking that studying God's Word is not for you because you're not a pastor. Remember, we want our progress to be evident to all. Paul prays for the believers at Colossae that their progress would be evident...

> Colossians 1:9-10 For this cause we also, since the day we heard it, do not cease to pray for you, and to

desire that ye might be filled with the knowledge of his will in all wisdom and spiritual understanding; That ye might walk worthy of the Lord unto all pleasing, being fruitful in every good work, and increasing in the knowledge of God;   (Underline Mine)

The knowledge of his will in all wisdom and spiritual understanding leads to progress that is evident in at least three ways. Here they are straight from the verse.

1. A walk worthy of the Lord
2. Fruitful and useful in every good work
3. Increasing knowledge if God

Don't neglect the Word of God and don't neglect your gifts and abilities to share what you've learned. Timothy had been ministering the Word of God for some time, and his abilities had no doubt developed over that time. Somewhere in time, there was Timothy's first sermon. Just guessing now, but I'm going to say it is very likely that first sermon of Timothy's was not his best. Timothy grew with experience; for that matter, so did Paul.

Going back to the beginning of my bike riding experience, that first ride was not my best, I wasn't ready that day to tackle the sand pit. Remember, I didn't even know how to stop without jumping off. Do you swim? Was that first swim the best you've ever done? Unless it is the only time you swam, you undoubtedly got better. It is the same with ministry, sharing testimonies, teaching lessons, being a witness, or any other way God directs you to serve; as you serve in any area, you will gain abilities and improve.

I think of our dear friend who played piano for our youth group in Michigan. She could accompany a soloist while simultaneously talking to someone else about a totally different subject. Once I saw her play one song while looking at music from another song while answering a question about it, she never missed a note. It was one of the most incredible, yet subtle accomplishments I've ever seen. While she was totally amazing (she obviously had a special gift from God with that ability), we have to recognize that she also had to cultivate that talent and ability. As with the other areas of her life, with her music, she was all in for God. She knew God gave her that ability, and she used it for HIS purposes. Until the day she died, she glorified God with what He gave her.

To make sure we are practicing these things, we must take a close accounting to be sure we are doing what we set out to do, being committed to godliness, so that our progress is evident to all.

> 1 Timothy 4:16 Take heed unto thyself, and unto the doctrine; continue in them: for in doing this thou shalt both save thyself, and them that hear thee. (Underline Mine)

Take heed or take note is to pay attention. Timothy is to pay attention to himself and to his doctrine, the teaching of the Word of God. We don't want Timothy or ourselves to wander off course or lose focus. Pay attention to yourself to see if your indicators of the example of the believers are out there and functioning. It is so easy to fall into a 'do as I say, not as I do' attitude. That deceitful kind of example just doesn't lead people to Christlikeness.

First, our example has to be right. Are we actually living the life we talk about?

Then Timothy has to take heed to the doctrine. Doctrine is teaching, in this case Biblical teaching. When we share the Word of God, we have to make sure it is actually God's Word that we are sharing. Can we actually find the passage that we are talking about in the Bible? I think by now you've heard that 79% of all quoted statistics are made up on the spot, just like this one was. I made it up to emphasize a point; some people quote the Bible for credibility, even if the quote is not from the Bible.

Secondly, our Learning has to be right. Does it really reflect Biblical standards?

The message here is to stay on track, then continue. Keep teaching. Keep emphasizing God's Word. Keep living the example of the believers with all your indicators on. Practice these things and be committed to them so that when it comes to godliness, you will show obvious conduct.

[1]Warren W Wiersbe, 2007, The Wiersbe Bible Commentary NT, Pg761, David C Cook Publisher

Chapter Seven
Progress Produces Fruit

We are all given something from God, gifts and abilities, and we are all expected to have some return on the investment God has put into us. There should be fruit of the spirit apparent in our lives.

> Galatians 5:22-23 But the fruit of the Spirit is love, joy, peace, longsuffering, gentleness, goodness, faith, meekness, temperance: against such there is no law.

As Christians, we are expected to bear fruit for God as we discussed in the previous chapters 'that thy profiting may appear to all'. When we think of fruit, we automatically begin to think of farming. Jesus told an interesting parable in Matthew 13 that connects farming and growing crops with the condition of the soil the seeds are planted in. Before we read the parable, let's acknowledge that farmers routinely cultivate their land before they plant their seed into it.

In southwest lower Michigan where I am from, it is a big-time farming area. At times every year, it is very common to see tractors following tractors down the roads. You can't get anywhere without following a tractor at some point. It is also common to see huge piles of rocks of all sizes piled up in the corner of the fields, rocks that formerly cluttered up their fields. They actually sell their unwanted rocks to landscapers who use them as lawn decorations.

Once those seeds are planted in rows, the farmers can till the weeds under while not disturbing the crops they planted. Not having to share the nutrients and the moisture in the soil with the weeds means the crops have a better chance to produce a better yield. The point is that farmers put a lot of time into preparing the soil, so they can receive the greatest harvest possible. Jesus uses this parable in Matthew 13:1-8[1] then re-tells it in v18-23 with explanations.

> Matthew 13:18-23 Hear ye therefore the parable of the sower. When any one heareth the word of the kingdom, and understandeth it not, then cometh the wicked one, and catcheth away that which was sown in his heart. This is he which received seed by the way side. (Underline Mine)
>
> But he that received the seed into stony places, the same is he that heareth the word, and anon with joy receiveth it; Yet hath he not root in himself, but dureth for a while: for when tribulation or persecution ariseth because of the word, by and by he is offended.
>
> He also that received seed among the thorns is he that heareth the word; and the care of this world,

102

and the deceitfulness of riches, choke the word, and he becometh unfruitful.

But he that received seed into <u>the good ground</u> is he that heareth the word, and understandeth it; which also <u>beareth fruit</u>, and <u>bringeth forth, some an hundredfold, some sixty, some thirty</u>. (Underlines Mine)

The sower sows the seed representing the Word of God into the differing soils which represent the differing conditions of the human heart. The human race has every kind of heart in it from the hardest least likely to receive the Gospel to the most cultivated and tender heart that cannot wait to hear from God's Word. We are all somewhere between those two extremes.

I have personally witnessed to people with hardened and calloused hearts of bad soil and seen them repent in a moment crying out to God for salvation and new life; their hardened heart was changed. While the soil of the wayside is hard and trampled, it can crack. I think of the sidewalk in front of our house in Johannesburg. The sidewalk itself is in very passable shape, dozens of dozens people walk it every day. Still there are cracks in the sidewalk that are growing grass. About every two weeks, I have to go out there and mow the sidewalk. I could (if the city would let me) go out there and break up the sidewalk and remove the debris to plant strawberries or carrots. That strip of land would change and yield fruit. The determining factor in the change of the sidewalk is me and my back; the determining factor of the change in a heart is the work of Jesus Christ and our acceptance of Him.

In this parable, I cannot say that all these examples are of saved people. In fact, most of the people represented by these soils never repent and stay as they are, fruitless, useless, and unsaved. The good soil that bears fruit represents the saved people. By the parable, we see that there is a soil (or a field) that yields a <u>good</u> 30 fold increase, one that yields a <u>better</u> 60 fold increase, and one that yields a <u>best</u> 100 fold return. People move from one of the fruitless soils to a fruitful soil by trusting Christ for salvation. Also, it doesn't have to be 30, 60, or 100 fold. People are all over the spectrum. The point is there will be fruit somewhere at some time in every believer's life.

We have led homeless people to the Lord at rescue missions from time to time in our ministry. These were hardened guys who had been in and out of jail multiple times who in some cases never knew Jesus Christ was a person and not just an exclamation. Other times, we have led teenagers to the Lord who were mixed up in worldly things to the point that they are getting in trouble at school and with the law. At the early age of 14 or 15, they would already be characterized as hardened by the world. Then there is the kid who ignores God because he is a good person. Sometimes these kinds are more difficult because their heart is hardened by pride; we've led them to the Lord also. That change is by God through His Holy Spirit.

As we would share God's Word their hardened hearts would crack, and they would trust Jesus Christ with their eternal destiny. When these hard hearted people get saved I like to watch when they pray. Many times you will see a single tear, or they will wipe their eyes before the tear is visible. That is a sign of a repentant heart; which is fruit. Anytime I lead someone to the Lord for salvation, I like to ask how they feel right then; immediately after they trusted Jesus for salvation. Very commonly, they have a feeling of peace. However, it is a peace that they cannot explain; like nothing they have ever felt before. That is the peace of God that passes all understanding -- which is fruit.

When the hardened heart is changed by God's Word, the soil is just broken up a little bit. There is still a huge amount of debris in their life that has to be cleaned up.

> Psalms 10:17 LORD, thou hast heard the desire of the humble: thou wilt prepare their heart, thou wilt cause thine ear to hear:

Sinners come to Christ with the baggage of the destructiveness of their sin. That doesn't all go away overnight. Salvation is accomplished immediately, but the process of developing a godly walk takes time, and it requires work. Through our salvation and our willingness to become more like Christ, we want to do this work of fruitfulness, but we have to acknowledge it is work.

Now thinking again about those verses in Matthew 13, there was soil that produced a good return of fruit, a soil that produced a better return of fruit, and a soil that produced the best return of fruit. If you equate the soil of your heart to this model, it would only make sense to try to be the soil with the kind of heart attitude of the best producing soil. We would then have to cultivate the soil of our heart, renewing our mindset by knowing and following God's Word, by developing the kind of indicators of the example of the believers, and by walking worthy of the Lord as we've been talking about in this book.

If you're saved, there is going to be fruit somewhere in your life...

> Matthew 7:17-20 Even so every good tree bringeth forth good fruit; but a corrupt tree bringeth forth evil fruit. A good tree cannot bring forth evil fruit, neither can a corrupt tree bring forth good fruit. Every tree that bringeth not forth good fruit is hewn down, and cast into the fire. Wherefore by their fruits ye shall know them.

Through the fruits of the Spirit listed in Galatians 5:22-23, we can expect to see holiness developing. We talked about this as 'purity' in the previous chapter. In fact, the Galatians Fruit of the Spirit list leads us to a godly temperament or character; fruit unto holiness that ends up in our everlasting life.

> Romans 6:22 But now being made free from sin, and become servants to God, ye have your fruit unto holiness, and the end everlasting life.

Through the fruits of the Spirit listed in Galatians 5:22-23, we can expect to see the fruits of a close walk with the Lord that is worthy and pleasing to Him, fruitful and growing in the good cultivated soil of your heart.

> Colossians 1:10 That ye might walk worthy of the Lord unto all pleasing, being fruitful in every good work, and increasing in the knowledge of God;

The fruit of the increasing knowledge of God and a walk worthy of Him commonly manifests itself in preaching or witnessing (or both). Paul was an evangelist preacher who had such a close walk with God and an increasing knowledge of Him that he could not help but tell others about the saving grace of Jesus Christ. Being a faithful witness of Christ is a fruit of a heart where the soil has been carefully cultivated.

> Romans 1:13 Now I would not have you ignorant, brethren, that oftentimes I purposed to come unto you... that I might have some fruit among you also...

Praise is a common outpouring of the fruit of the lips of a cultivated and fruitful heart of humility towards God and man.

> Hebrews 13:15 By him therefore let us offer the sacrifice of praise to God continually, that is, the fruit of our lips giving thanks to his name.

All of these are evidence that God has made a change in your hearts condition based on your faith in Him. Any

Christian (with some cultivation, care, and pruning) can turn into a useful and fruitful Christian.

You will have obvious conduct, and you really can behave like an example of the believer!

[1]Matthew 13:1-8 The same day went Jesus out of the house, and sat by the sea side. And great multitudes were gathered together unto him, so that he went into a ship, and sat; and the whole multitude stood on the shore. And he spake many things unto them in parables, saying, Behold, a sower went forth to sow; And when he sowed, some seeds fell by the way side, and the fowls came and devoured them up: Some fell upon stony places, where they had not much earth: and forthwith they sprung up, because they had no deepness of earth: And when the sun was up, they were scorched; and because they had no root, they withered away. And some fell among thorns; and the thorns sprung up, and choked them: But other fell into good ground, and brought forth fruit, some an hundredfold, some sixtyfold, some thirtyfold.

Appendix 1
The Prerequisite

This book is about how to live the authentic Christian life that God meant for us. The obvious prerequisite to living a Christian life is being a Christian. Many people today believe they are a Christian because of the country they live in or the family they are from. That false belief has come about over time but is not rooted in the Scriptures. Scripture tells us the Gospel or good news of Jesus Christ is the pathway to salvation.

> 1 Corinthians 15:1-4 Moreover, brethren, I declare unto you the gospel which I preached unto you, which also ye have received, and wherein ye stand; By which also ye are saved, if ye keep in memory what I preached unto you, unless ye have believed in vain. For I delivered unto you first of all that which I also received, how that Christ died for our sins according to the scriptures; And that he was buried, and that he rose again the third day according to the scriptures: (Underline Mine)

The term Christian literally comes from the Greek to mean 'Little Christs'. A 'Little Christ' is someone who has put all of their trust in Jesus alone and His finished work on the cross for their salvation from their sins. In the early days of Christianity, the thought was to strive to be like Christ. Christians firstly trust or believe that Jesus died and rose again in victory over death to save us from our sins; our faith placed in Him to save us is where we become Christian. Then because of the gratitude of our thankfulness, we want to be transformed to be like Him and share in His attributes as a 'Little Christ' thus living a life that honors Him.

My favorite verses that concisely show this progression are found in Ephesians.

> Ephesians 2:8-10 For by grace are ye <u>saved through faith</u>; and that not of yourselves: it is the gift of God: Not of works, lest any man should boast. For we are his workmanship, created in Christ Jesus unto good works, which God hath before ordained that we should walk in them. (Underline Mine)

Why do I need salvation? I'm a pretty good person! Well, let's look at that for a minute. Be honest with yourself and admit the truth. Have you ever lied? Have you ever stolen anything, even an ink pen or a paper clip? Have you ever helped someone else cover up their sin or looked the other way pretending you didn't know? Sure, you're a sinner just like I am. We all are; in fact, the Bible says so too.

> Romans 3:10 As it is written, There is none righteous, no, not one:

Romans 3:23 For all have sinned, and come short of the glory of God;

Here is a verse I use in Chapter 3: Renew Your View.

Isaiah 64:6 But we are all as an unclean thing, and all our righteousness's are as filthy rags; and we all do fade as a leaf; and our iniquities, like the wind, have taken us away.

Our 'iniquities' are our sins, and they have taken us away, away from God. Our sins have created a separation between us and God that we cannot overcome on our own. That is why Jesus came and died for us; each of us. Jesus came as a man and a man like us. He was born like us, had to physically develop like us, and became as we are. At the same time, Jesus is the eternal God. I cannot explain all of that to you, but that is Jesus Christ the God-Man.

Why couldn't God just fix sin? Why did Jesus have to die?

Romans 6:23a For the wages of sin is death...

Because God does not take short cuts. Jesus had to die for my sin, or I had to die for my sin. That is the payment for the sins that we do. Ok, that is good for me; Jesus died for my sin. It is a fair exchange, one sinless man dying for one sinner. What about the others of you that want to go to Heaven someday? Does Jesus have to die once for each of us? Thankfully, no! Remember Jesus is the God-Man, a man like we are to die for man, and infinite God to die for an infinite number of people.

Romans 5:6-9 For when we were yet without strength, in due time <u>Christ died for the ungodly</u>. For scarcely for a righteous man will one die: yet peradventure for a good man some would even dare to die. But God commendeth his love toward us, in that, while we were yet sinners, <u>Christ died for us</u>. Much more then, <u>being now justified by his blood, we shall be saved</u> from wrath through him. (Underlines Mine)

We are justified by His shed blood. God loved us enough to die in our place! God sent His Son Jesus so that we could place our faith and trust in Him and not have to face the wages of our sin.

John 3:16-18 For God so loved the world, that he gave his only begotten Son, that <u>whosoever believeth in him</u> (Jesus) <u>should not perish, but have everlasting life</u>. For God sent not his Son into the world to condemn the world; <u>but that the world through him might be saved</u>. He that believeth on him is not condemned: but he that believeth not is condemned already, because he hath not believed in the name of the only begotten Son of God. (Parenthesis & Underlines Mine)

God through His Son Jesus Christ has done everything necessary for you to be saved. Whoever you are and wherever you are, all you have to do is place all your faith and trust in Jesus alone to save you. He wants your free-will trust and acceptance, which is your faith.

If you've never done anything like this before, take the next step and believe Him. Then, tell Him your decision. Yes, He already knows, but it will benefit you to pray and talk to God about your trusting faith in His Son.

> Romans 10:9-10 That if thou shalt confess with thy mouth the Lord Jesus, and shalt believe in thine heart that God hath raised him from the dead, thou shalt be saved. For with the heart man believeth unto righteousness; and with the mouth confession is made unto salvation.

Pray something like this... Dear Jesus, I know I have sinned, and I'm sorry. Please forgive me. The wage for my sins is death. I understand that You died for me, and I want to accept Your sacrifice on my behalf. I am trusting in You Jesus, and You alone to save me and take me to Heaven when I die. I want to learn to serve You in my life. I want to learn to be like You. Thank You for loving me so much. Now, I want to love You! I ask for your help, and I thank You for what You have done. In Your name Jesus, I pray. Amen.

If you've done something like that in the sincerity of your heart, trusting Christ to save you, would you please tell someone? Maybe someone gave you this book, if so, they would like to hear about your decision. Tell a friend, tell a parent, or tell me at mike.obviouschoices@gmail.com

Once you've done that, begin learning more and more about God and His Word, the Bible. If you came to this section from Chapter One, then go back to Chapter Two and finish reading!

Made in the USA
Columbia, SC
21 July 2017